Diary of a Pregnant Dad

Diary of a Pregnant Dad

Rob Wilcher

HADDINGTON PRESS

First published in 2004
Reprinted 2005

Haddington Press Pty Ltd
Box 3182, Domain Road P. O.
South Yarra, Victoria 3141
Phone: (61 3) 9866 2758
Fax: (61 3) 9866 2751
Email: haddingtonpress@bigpond.com
Website: www.haddingtonpress.com.au

National Library of Australia
Cataloguing-in-Publication entry:

Wilcher, Rob, 1961– .

Diary of a pregnant dad: the essential monthly guide from
conception to birth for every father-to-be.

ISBN 0 9751680 0 2.

1. Pregnancy – Miscellanea. 2. Childbirth. 3. Fathers. 1. Title.

618.2

Text and cover design by Andrew Cunningham – Studio Pazzo
Illustrations by Caitlin Murray
Printed by Everbest in China

10 9 8 7 6 5 4 3 2

To those special people who made me a father –
Sophie, Mirari and Amare. To fathers everywhere.
And to Tigerlili (woof!).

Acknowledgements

I'd like to thank Sophie for encouraging me to write it, and for giving me the subject matter, all those who helped type the manuscript outside work hours – Helen, Elizabeth, Karen, Marion, Jenny, Beryl and others (what luxury!), Michael Webster for stepping up to check the medical material, Patti Miller for a general thumbs up on the assessment, all those who test read the manuscript - David, Paul, Susan, Karen, Frances, Glenn and others, to Paul and Georgina for having faith in the manuscript (our first baby!), Jen, Andrew and Caitlin for making it look good, numerous friends who bounced ideas and stories around, and let me use some of them (bless you all), Tigerlili, who has suffered on the pecking order, and Mirari and Amare, for being so utterly wonderful (I am in love). I think that's everybody.

Introduction

When my wife told me she was pregnant, and all the hoo-hah had died down (a bit), I figured it would be good to know what pregnancy might mean from the man's point of view. So I went looking for a book that would give me a feel for what I was about to go through. I wanted to hear how someone else's perceptions of fatherhood developed during the pregnancy as he geared up for the birth. How did he prepare himself? What took him by surprise? How did the pregnancy affect his relationship with the mother? How did he deal with things like mood swings and morning sickness? Those sorts of issues . . .

But that kind of book didn't exactly jump off the shelf. There are a zillion books on pregnancy and childbirth, all with one thing in common: they're primarily aimed at mothers. Which is fair enough really. A lot is going to happen to them. That fact, however, means a lot is going to happen to the fathers too, but oddly, books aimed at fathers-to-be are thin on the ground. I wasn't asking for anything technical or too detailed, I could get all that from the mothers' books. I just wanted one man's story, with some introductory information about the baby's development and a bit of anecdotal advice to help me understand what the mother's going through.

When I realised I wasn't going to find my ideal book, I decided to write it myself: a warts and all, front-line view of the baby-making game, from kick off through to delivery time. So here it is. My own baby, if you like.

A couple of things I have to say before we start. First, as every pregnancy book (in fact every mother, every gynaecologist, obstetrician, nurse, midwife, parent and pamphlet) will tell you, every pregnancy and birth is unique. It means of course that every father also has a different experience of the whole thing. There are no real rules as to how this game is played. There are only rules of thumb, best used as a sounding board for each person's experience. Rules of thumb as general as: labour is painful (although some women don't have much pain), her belly will get bigger (although you wouldn't know it with some women until the very last moment), her breasts will get bigger (ditto), she'll either lose interest in sex or become really horny, and the end product is always a human being (although fifteen years later this may be doubtful).

Second, what I know about medicine wouldn't cover a beer mat. I'm just an average worker with a wife, a mortgage and a family (yay!). So I asked our obstetrician, Dr Michael Webster, to help me understand the technical stuff, although if there are any mistakes in this book, they're not his fault. Dr Webster has been practising as a gynaecologist and obstetrician for over twenty years, is a Fellow of the Royal Australian and New Zealand College of Obstetricians and Gynaecologists, and also a Fellow of the Royal College of Obstetricians and Gynaecologists in the United Kingdom. So he knows what he's talking about. He's also a dad. So he really knows what he's talking about.

Here we go then ... and hang on to your hat: it's the greatest ride of your life.

Contents

In the beginning

a positive result!

What's happening to me

THE NEWS

It's 4.00 am. I'm awake, tossing and turning with a busy mind full of problems at work, what to buy people for Christmas, what I should get Mum to buy me for Christmas, and . . . Ruby (my wife's a redhead) is awake too. She shuffles and turns, then sighs.

'Are you awake?' I ask, hoping to be diverted with an early morning chat. Or something more. 'I feel disgusting,' I hear her say.

No chance of that then.

'Really disgusting,' she adds.

Absolutely none.

'My period's late. I'm nauseous. You know how tired I've been. I think I'm pregnant.'

What? Pregnant! Now I'm awake. I raise myself on to my elbow and look at her dark form silhouetted by the street lights outside. She's moving her hands across her stomach.

'Pregnant?'

She turns her head towards me. 'It's going to be a girl,' she says. 'I can tell.'

'How?' I ask.

'I just can,' she replies. She shuffles a bit and sighs. 'I'll go to the chemist in the morning and get a test kit.' And with that she rolls over. She's still for a while. It looks like she's asleep.

'Are you asleep?' I whisper.

'Go to sleep,' she murmurs. I caress her side and she holds my hand.

Pregnant. Wow. Like I'm going to get to sleep now. Pregnant! Of course she might not be. She might just be sick. End of year blues, work, family, me, health, holiday ... the baby. The baby? If she is pregnant, what exactly is 'it' now? An embryo? A foetus? Four cells? How big? I guess it must be tiny. And how pregnant is she? One week? Two? Ten? When do you notice? How soon can she tell? If it's so tiny, how can she be so sure? Or is this the famous feminine intuition? She just knows, intuitively, physically, that (a) she's pregnant and (b) it's a girl.

Okay, pregnant I can accept. I'll grant it's possible for Ruby to know intuitively she's pregnant, but a girl? How could she know the gender? When does a foetus or embryo or whatever it is become a gender? I know that the character of the sperm determines the sex (like the character of the sex determines sperm) but she couldn't possibly know yet what sex the sperm has determined. And besides . . .

Hang on a minute. Pregnant! That means . . . I'm going to be a father. Call me quick off the mark, but it's just hit me. I'm going to be a father! Wow! Oo-er! Yeehah! Me, a father. I've fathered a child with Ruby. We're going to be parents. Awesome.

I look at her. I can hear her rhythmic breathing, and the outlines of her features are slightly more clear in the promise of early morning light. She's fast asleep, or looks like it. Wow. Pregnant. Maybe Mum should buy me something 'parental' for Christmas like a cot or a pram, or some toys – a ball or something. Hang on, that's way too far ahead. The kid's not even a kid yet, let alone big enough to kick a ball around. Maybe I should think about work again. It's 5.00 am. Pregnant. I go to sleep.

And that's how it was. The first I heard about it. The first inkling of things to come, in the wee small hours of the morning.

Wow.

Pregnant.

Me. A father.

Awesome.

TESTING THE NEWS

When I awoke it was a sunny Saturday morning. Light streamed in through the bedroom window. I leant over to give Ruby a hug, but she wasn't there. The sheets on her side of the bed lay open and cold. I thought she must have gone to the chemist already. I lay there thinking good thoughts about her, staring at a long red strand curled on the pillow. She came into the bedroom carrying a pillow and wearing nothing but a grumpy look on her face.

'Been to the chemist?' I asked. Dumb question really, given the scanty outfit.

'No,' she mumbled, 'in the spare room. Your snoring kept me awake.' She slumped into the bed next to me. 'You've got to go back to Anthony'. Anthony was an acupuncturist Ruby sent me to a year ago to stop me snoring.

'It's only temporary,' I pleaded. 'It's stress. I'll relax over the Christmas break.' She grunted in reply. Anthony, I remembered, had once told Ruby that if he was present at her labour he could give her a pain-free delivery.

After a while she sat up and said, 'I'd better go to the chemist.'

'How are you feeling?' I asked her.

She raised an eyebrow in my direction. 'Aside from lack of sleep?'

'You looked asleep,' I said.

She glared at me accusingly, and muttered, 'I was. You woke me.'

'Aside from lack of sleep then,' I said, hoping to move the discussion forward.

'Disgusting, but a bit better than before.'

'And what you said last night?' I asked.

She was almost dressed now. She said, 'About being pregnant? Let's see what the test says.'

I sat up on the end of the bed. 'Do you want me to come with you?'

'No, you stay in bed.'

'Sure?'

'Uh-huh,' and she was gone. I opened a book and had a bit of a read. Tiger, our dog, jumped on to the bed and arranged herself sumptuously in a pool of sunlight, her head peering out the window into the street where Ruby had gone.

About twenty minutes later when Ruby returned, Tiger bounded off the bed, her tail wagging frantically. I saw them both pass the bedroom door in a jumble of brown fur and white plastic shopping bags.

'What are all the bags for?' I asked. 'Just how many test kits did you buy?'

'We needed some stuff,' she called from the end of the house.

We needed some stuff? She suspects she's pregnant and she goes out shopping for groceries? I wouldn't have gone shopping for anything else. What's happening here? Is she trying to avoid the inevitable? I heard her rustling in the kitchen. The fridge opened and closed, opened and closed again, accompanied by the pattering of dog's paws on the wooden floor. How can she be so calm? I would have gone straight to the test kit first.

'Are we going to do this thing?' I called, getting impatient.

'What?'

'Did you get the test kit?' I called back.

'I'll do it in a minute,' she replied.

In a minute! We're about to test for the most life-changing event we will probably ever undergo, and she says she'll do it in a minute. Finally I heard her step into the bathroom. 'Do you want a hand?' I asked, trying to sound helpful.

'I'm weeing on the stick thing,' she shouted. 'There's not a whole lot you can do.'

Well, that was the truth. We'd had a scare (if that's the word) earlier in the year. She'd been late. The kit she used then had required her to urinate into a glass and dip the tester into the glass after 30 seconds or so. I'd bought a double kit and we sat on the bed together holding hands, our bodies touching and hearts thumping, but it was negative on both tests. Which was according to plan at the time. We'd intended to have a last overseas trip together next year and then start trying for a family when we got back. But no, it looked like we were in for a different trip. This time I stayed in bed and waited for the test result, not wanting to create too much anticipation in case it was negative again. Which would also have been according to plan. There was (dare I say it) a pregnant silence as I waited for her to announce the results of the test. She entered the bedroom and looked at me with an intense yet slightly glazed smile. Between the forefinger and thumb of one hand she held the end of a white plastic instrument.

'Well?' I asked.

'I think I'm pregnant.'

I sat up quickly. 'What do you mean "think"?'

'You wee straight on to this thing,' she said. 'If two bars appear then you're pregnant, but the second bar isn't very strong. Here, have a look.' She sat on the bed next to me and handed me the tester. 'See if you can work it out,' she said.

It was a plastic stick a bit like a text highlighter with a felt tip, all white but for two blue stripes across the end. Two clear blue stripes. Powder blue. Sky blue. On a cloud white tester. Sure, one was a lighter blue than the other, but there was no mistaking it. Two clear, blue, pregnant stripes.

'It says on the box that it's 99 per cent accurate,' said Ruby.

We sat together on the edge of the bed while the realisation of it swept through us, looking first at the tester, then the floor, then the wardrobe and then each other. Before I knew it had begun, an enormous smile stretched across my face. Ruby was wearing a generous, joyous, girlish happy grin. I put my arms around her. We hugged very close for a while, holding the damp end of the tester away from us like a religious icon.

'This is it, then,' I remember blurting out and immediately wondered if it was a silly thing to say. She pulled away a bit, her eyes glistening with tears, kissed me and shrank back into my arms, holding me close in a strong, emotion-charged embrace. The familiar fragrance of her hair filled my nose.

This is one of those great moments in life, I thought, so great that it felt like every thought and every possibility was reeling around inside my head. Greater than graduating from school or uni or college, greater than buying a house, or a milestone birthday, like a twenty-first. Greater even than getting married. We had agreed before we tied the knot – before we got serious – that we wanted to have children, and now it was happening, or about to. The culmination of marriage. Something far greater. This was LOVE. This was me being a father, Ruby a mother, and us joining together to make a real live thing, part me, part her, wholly – if it had any self yet – itself.

So I stood by the bed in just a T-shirt, clutching a urine-soaked tester in one hand and squeezing my wife very close with the other hand feeling intense surges of love and pride and happiness and smelling her hair and looking at the floor and thinking that any moment now the ends of my ever-broadening smile were going to meet at the back of my scalp and the top part of my head was going to flip off like the lid of a boiled breakfast egg.

We sat together on the edge of the bed while the realisation of it swept through us, looking first at the tester, then the floor, then the wardrobe and then each other. Before I knew it had begun, an enormous smile stretched across my face.

At moments like these words are so totally meaningless and yet so full of meaning that they burst under their own weight. So when I pried Ruby from my arms (carefully avoiding contact with the wee-wee end of the tester), looked deep into her glistening eyes and inanely said, 'Mother,' she said something like 'Ummm' and reburied her head in my chest. I've never understood why women cry – genuinely cry – when they are happy. But they do. Maybe not all of them but every one I've come across. I announced proudly, 'I've never got a woman pregnant before.'

Ruby laughed and looked up at me. She stroked my face with her fingers and said, 'Sweet man', which always gets me going. She told me she loved me. Then it was on for young and old with kisses, hugs, gropes, octopus hands up under my T-shirt, across my thighs and just when things looked like we might re-enact the moment of conception she said, 'I feel disgusting', turned away with her nervous half-laugh, and padded off towards the kitchen.

I was left standing in the bedroom with no pants on, three-quarters aroused but fast deflating, head brimming with impending fatherhood, heart pounding with the twin forces of goodwill and grandeur, smelling of sleep and grinning from ear to ear like a village idiot. Through the fog inside my brain I heard a voice from the kitchen saying, 'Do you want some toast?' I pulled on a pair of shorts and headed out to the sounds of knife sawing bread. I curled my arms around her and Tiger joined in by jumping up on to my hips, digging her pointed claws into my skin. Ruby held the bread knife out of harm's way like a wet pregnancy tester which I suddenly realised had gone missing in all the emotion of the moment.

'It's in the bin,' she said in a matter-of-fact way. Which is fair enough when you think about it (and it needn't bear much thinking about). It's not the kind of thing you'd frame and keep for posterity like gilded baby boots, or the stills from the first ultrasound, and before I had a chance to block it out, an awful challenge leered at me from the future. Would I become one of those fathers who joyously videoed everything about his child? Everything from the moment the purple head emerges into the light amidst the screams of labour? Or who posts footage of the first crawl, the first step, the first word, on the new family website?

The truth was, I had to admit, I found the idea attractive. For the first time, I appreciated the sentiment behind the lust for keepsakes and mementos. New feelings of pride and love were building. This was my child, and I wanted to capture the total experience of it, so that I could look at a record in the years to come and revel in the memories, and demonstrate to my child how wonderful he(she) was.

It's all a bit nerdy really, especially when taken to extremes. I remembered there was a Norwegian medico who had developed pictures of the fertilisation and subsequent development of an embryo. And a couple of friends were undergoing the IVF thing and saw their fertilised eggs under the microscope with only eight cells each. I wondered if they had photographs. After just ten minutes into being a father I knew that I wanted to follow the details of what was happening very closely: the germination, birth and subsequent development of my child. All of a sudden I was feeling paternal and protective.

THE INEVITABLE QUESTION

Over tea and toast questions began flooding in. How pregnant was she? That depends on when we conceived. (We? She? Who does the conceiving?) Ideally, we would have known exactly the time and place when it happened. We would have planned it. We would have agreed that, this time, we will dock the fighter craft on the mother ship, we will lead the horse to water and make it drink, we will mix our marital metaphors in the happy grammar of love, and it will be a passionately unforgettable embrace of two procreative souls about which we could joyfully boast to the future offspring when she (he) is old enough to understand these things: 'You see, kid, you were conceived out of love. It was like this – I looked at your mother . . .'

As if.

But we hadn't planned it. Not precisely anyway. We were thinking of starting a family after our return from the planned holiday, so we'd stopped all tangible forms of contraception, just in case Ruby's body wanted a break from intervention before it began breeding. We were relying on the withdrawal method. No prizes for guessing how reliable that was. So I had no idea what time Ruby had conceived, and could only look back and guess on which of our many days and nights of passion the deed was finally done. The Sunday morning lie-ins? The Saturday afternoon sessions? The morning quickies? That evening on the dining room table? Sunday nights on the couch during the ad breaks? *En plein air* in the National Park? Celebrating the Aussies win over the West Indies? In the Edwardian splendour of the Carrington Hotel at Katoomba? On the rocks on a Bondi evening? On the car bonnet at the top of the Brooklyn safety ramp on a sunny Saturday afternoon? Caught in a thunder storm in Centennial Park? Or on Qantas flight QF 240 . . .

As if.

There are some women who immediately know when it happens. One friend said her second pregnancy was like the first: a sudden wave of emotion washed through her and she knew. Another said she knew the next day because she was 'just really happy inside'. But no man I know has ever been able to say on the occasion, or on the day after, that he knew his partner was pregnant. At best we just feel good for having got some. And besides, Ruby hadn't claimed any early intuition. She'd worked it out from feeling sick and tired over the last few weeks, along with a strange feeling in her tummy. So which time was it?

'I think it was the night at the Carrington,' said Ruby.

Aaah yes, the night of the Carrington, I mused as I munched on a piece of toast and jam. We had driven up one evening for a weekend treat, dined at Lindsay's on the main street of Katoomba with a luscious bottle of red and retired to the plush opulence of the Carrington Hotel. We watched James Bond – *Dr No* – while we finished the wine and drifted into satiated slumber. In the morning we made love: a languid sensual union, drowsy in the fragrance of each other's bodies, the entanglement of desire, the deep passion and mutual ecstasy of orgasm. I had been tender, strong and loving, she teasing and yielding. We'd done everything right. Yes, without doubt, the Carrington. What was it about that time that made Ruby pick then as the moment of conception?

'The maths,' she replied. 'I had my period about two weeks before and we hadn't had sex for a while. We girls only get a window of opportunity for ovulation – about a week or so – so it was probably then. Besides, that coincides with when I started feeling lethargic.' Then, rubbing salt into the wound, she added, 'We *did* have sex that weekend, didn't we?'

So that's the fact of it. Mathematics, ovulation, sperm meeting egg, lethargy, nausea and pregnancy. The prosaic physicality of when and how. Romance?

As if.

I spent the rest of the weekend with that big goofy grin on my face. My little swimmers had made their mark – or one of them at least, and I grinned with pride at their achievement. Several times throughout the day, Ruby would hug me and say something like 'I'm proud to be carrying your child', and my knees would tremble with admiration, devotion, and soul-expanding joy. Occasionally I'd see glimpses of the future – images of nappies, sleep deprivation, teenage angst – but I'd brush them aside in my fog of happiness. I don't know if other people noticed. Heaven only knows what they thought.

RESEARCH

I decided that one of the first things I could do to help Ruby was to find out all about pregnancy and how it works. To begin with, I'd buy some books on the subject: that way I could talk knowledgeably about what she would be going through, and be able to share in some of her experiences over the next nine months. I started at some major city book stores. Books on pregnancy were in the health section, just next to the sex manuals and guides to good loving. Which I thought was kind of appropriate: you follow the sex section and end up at pregnancy.

Predictably, there were shelves of books looking at pregnancy and childbirth from every conceivable angle (no pun intended): *How to Get Pregnant* (In Case You Haven't Worked it Out Yet), *Tantric Childbirth* (the Bestselling Sequel to Tantric Sex), *A Guide to Getting It On During Pregnancy, Birth the Yoga Way, Acupuncture and Pain Free Labour*. And so on. Photos of bulging healthy tummies and serene looking mothers beamed out from book covers, surrounded by baby items and cuddly toys in pastel shades of pink and blue.

The first thing that struck me was that there was no book written from the man's perspective. All the books were aimed at the mothers. How to stay thin while pregnant, how to stay happy while pregnant, how to stay fit while pregnant, how to do your hair while pregnant, how to have a career while pregnant. And so on. How to be the Absolute Superwoman While You are Pregnant. It was a lesson in the fact that this adventure is largely the woman's thing. So much is going to happen to her that's never going to happen to me. We men are out of the picture, sidelined for the next nine months. This was secret women's business and we weren't supposed to find out too much about it. We'd done our bit and should dip out. We'd dumped our load, and should disappear for nine months, leaving this pregnancy business to the womenfolk.

That had to change. With all the pressure these days on fathers to be as involved as possible I would have thought there was room for at least one book on what's happening to us. I wasn't looking for the *Men's Complete Guide to Pregnancy*, or *The Complete Analysis of the Physical Aspects of Child Bearing and Labour*. Nor was I looking for the male equivalent of the female-oriented books available: *How Your Wife/Partner got Pregnant, Best Yoga Positions While Your Wife/Partner Delivers Your Kid, Acupuncture to Relieve Your Pain While Your Wife/Partner Delivers Your Kid* . . .

I grabbed a passing store assistant and asked her advice. She pegged me straightaway. 'Are you going to be a dad?'

I shrugged, 'I don't know. When are you supposed to go public on these things?'

She smiled, and pulled a couple of books off the shelf. 'There isn't really anything specifically for men. But these are some of the regulars, which most women find helpful.' The books I bought (and yes we did find them helpful) were:

What to Expect When You're Expecting by Arlene Eisenberg, Heidi Markoff and Sandee Hathaway, (Cornstalk Books, 1999).
Month by month, it provides answers to a huge range of fears and questions that come up such as what's the best diet for pregnancy and how bad does vomiting have to be before you go to the doctor. A great reference book.
Up the Duff by Kaz Cooke, (Viking/Penguin, 1999).
A humorous week by week description of events. Some women love it,

some hate it. We loved it. A good initial source-book for the lay person and a great antidote to the cutesy-coo bollocks that often accompanies the childbirth industry.

The New Pregnancy and Childbirth by Sheila Kitzinger, (Doubleday, 1997). One of the main bibles of the childbirth genre, it contains the only real section on what men might be thinking about the whole deal. Sheila, as I later discovered, is one of the matriarchs of natural childbirth. Worth a read.

These books are written for the most part by women, and for women. Which is fair enough. That doesn't mean men shouldn't take a gander. If we can read her *Cleo* or *Cosmo*, then we can read these, although be warned, there aren't too many articles on outdoor sex or stick girls modelling swimsuits.

I also bought a ball-point pen and a pad of paper and went home to Ruby with a concept for a book. She thought it was a great idea.

'I've never written a book before,' I said.

'I've never had a baby before,' she replied. 'We'll see which is harder.'

Some months later I did come across a book for blokes, called *So You're Going to be a Dad*, by Peter Downey, (Simon and Schuster, 1994). It contains a bunch of stuff which men might find helpful, such as what not to say during the labour, and is another tale of the pregnancy from our side of the gender fence.

WHEN AND WHO TO TELL

We had friends over for dinner that night, so I bought a bottle of champagne to celebrate. Ruby said she couldn't possibly drink champagne tonight, she felt so disgusting and besides, she'd prefer to tell our families before friends. Also, if she was right about the dates, she was only four to five weeks pregnant and wasn't it customary to wait three months before you told everyone?

When and who to tell is a problematic issue. Family normally has first dibs. We wanted to tell the whole world as soon as we found out she was pregnant (and after all, the test kit said 99 per cent accurate). It's common not to go public until after the first *trimester*, as the first three months are the trickiest for the growing embryo, and most miscarriages occur in that period. So if you tell everyone and lose it in the first few months then you get to tell everyone you've lost it. Which is no fun. Best to tell no-one, then no-one will know if you lose it.

But a close friend of mine I call 'Guru Dave', had a different approach. Guru Dave and I go a long way back, and have spent many hours in pubs and cafes mulling over life, love, and the mysteries of the opposite sex. He always seems to come up with a new angle on things. His view on telling people about pregnancies (based on his own experience as a parent), was that you should tell anybody you want to as soon as you find out. Talk about it – it's a happy time. And if you lose it, it means you've got some friends to help you through the grief. There's no shame in grieving about it. Otherwise, if you've told no-one, then no-one will know you've lost it, and you'll suffer in solitude. Which really is no fun.

So we agreed to tell the family first, and maybe one or two special friends. Ruby sat on one drink that night, gave me half her dinner because it tasted funny, and the champers stayed unopened in the fridge.

FEELING DISGUSTING – THE CRAVINGS

The next day, Sunday, we'd planned a day's walk in the Blue Mountains. But when I asked Ruby if she still wanted to go she replied, 'I feel too disgusting,' rolled over and went back to sleep. I figured this would be a phrase I would be hearing quite often: the notorious morning sickness. (When I first heard this expression as a child I thought it was 'mourning' sickness because women complained of feeling sick all day long, not just the morning. What troubled me then was why such a happy event inspired a time of mourning!)

'Can I get you anything?' I asked, again trying to be helpful.

'No,' she replied glumly.

'Cup of tea?'

'No.'

'Piece of toast?'

'I feel disgusting.'

I didn't want to push the issue, but I'd heard that pregnant women have strange cravings for things like abalone and chocolate pie or parsley ice cream so I added solicitously, 'Anything at all?'

'No. Nothing,' she said firmly.

Well, at least she hadn't thrown up yet, which was one consolation. It meant I was denied brownie points for holding her hair out of the bucket as she chucked. (Early in our relationship she'd had a bout of food poisoning, and I'd held her hair back out of the toilet bowl as she vomited. She said the experience had endeared me to her which only goes to show that you sure can't pick what attracts people to each other.) At least, I thought, I could record one point on the ledger by not insisting she eat. And, I wondered with naive male suspicion, is it possible that morning sickness is not a product of a growing embryo but the body's natural response to two kilograms of abalone and chocolate pie and a family-sized tub of parsley ice-cream? Obviously, I had a lot to learn. Discretion being the better part of valour, I left Ruby to feel disgusting, and trusted that if she needed something she would call and I would prove myself useful by answering. In the meantime I wondered whether I should stock up on abalone and chocolate just in case.

Later that morning Ruby traipsed out of the bedroom followed by Tiger. 'I feel disgusting,' she muttered as she headed to the bathroom. I waited, and cringed as I heard the unmistakable sounds of retching.

'Are you all right?' I called.

'Yes,' she called back and another guttural roar echoed from the porcelain. Brownie points time. I went into the bathroom and held her hair back as she crouched over the toilet bowl. Poor thing. She looked up. Her face was pale and drawn. She reached for the flush button and said, 'Matso dumpling soup.'

I wasn't quite sure I'd heard her correctly . . . was she telling me this was what she'd just seen in the toilet?

'Matso dumpling soup,' she repeated. 'That's what I can eat. You remember? I bought some for you when you had the flu. Matso dumpling soup.'

I hadn't predicted that. But there it was – matso dumpling soup.

'We're going to DB's,' she said and padded back into the bedroom to get dressed. DB's was a café in a nearby suburb that specialised in matso dumpling soup.

At the café she casually stirred the clear broth around the two newspaper-coloured tennis balls in her large white bowl. Then she brought the spoon to her mouth and slurped the soup noisily.

'This is good soup,' she said.

'Are you feeling any better?' I asked.

'No,' she replied, 'but it's good soup. I might have another one and order some to take home.' We hadn't actually told the proprietor that Ruby was pregnant but he must have twigged something was up. When he brought out the eight takeaway cartons of matso dumpling soup he added a free loaf of bread.

HOLIDAYS WITHOUT KIDS –
THE FIRST CASUALTY

Back at home, Ruby moaned, 'I can't go to Nepal.' We'd planned, paid for all the tickets and purchased a pile of equipment for a mountain trek in Nepal. We'd been training very hard over the last six months: long hours in the gym, up at 5.30 am to run along the beach, pounding up staircases, and down, and up (and down and up and down and up and down), push ups, weights, jogging, bush walking, etc. I was the fittest I'd been in fifteen years. I'd dropped a notch in my belt, bought new clothes, and – what was most amazing – had been getting up before 7.00 am to do – of all things – exercise. We'd booked to go to Kathmandu in three weeks, just in time for New Year's Eve before heading out to the mountains. It was to be our final fling together as DINKS (Double Income No Kids) before starting a family.

But junior had come along earlier than planned. We'd have to either cancel the trip, or at least transfer to one that wasn't so energetic. Ruby wouldn't be able to climb any 5,000-metre peaks, given that she was feeling disgusting. Even if it were physically possible for her to do the trip, we feared it might expose her to the risk of early miscarriage. The altitude might be dangerous for the embryo and if complications arose, we would be miles away from any medical attention. Besides, lugging a twenty kilogram pack up bloody great mountain sides in sub-zero temperatures is hard work at the best of times, but doing it with morning sickness would be, well, disgusting.

The next day, Monday, we advised the travel company of the pregnancy. Ruby obtained a note from the Travellers Medical Vaccination Centre advising that women who lived at sea level should not travel above 2,000 metres if pregnant where it was not necessary to do so. (Where was it necessary to do so, I wondered, except if you're Nepalese?) We thought we could change to a less strenuous trek, but the travel company told us that we were one day inside the 30-day cancellation period. As a result, we would lose all our booking fees – amounting to $11,000 – even though we could have advised them on the Saturday when we found out. No, they couldn't accommodate us. They had pre-paid all the agents in Nepal, and weren't able to refund any of our money, or even transfer us to another trek in Nepal. They simply couldn't help. We'd have to take it up with the travel insurance company.

The reality was we didn't have a hope. There was no way an insurance company would pay up for a glitch in the withdrawal method. We didn't stand a chance. The insurance company took one look at us and laughed.

Damn. But as it turned out, the travel company ended up being very generous, and repaid everything they hadn't prepaid, waiving their own legal rights. It still meant we were out of pocket, but not nearly as much as we'd expected. I made a mental note to book them in ten years time when M might be old enough to start trekking.

In the meantime Ruby had been to her GP to have our own 99 per cent accurate urine pregnancy kit results verified (or not, if we were one of the one per cent). The GP had her perform another urine sample. A similar test method. The same result. She sent me an email simply saying, 'Yes.'

Stupidly, I didn't get it at first and emailed back, 'Yes, what?'

She was too smart to reply and after half an hour it dawned on me that, by the authority of two urine tests and a GP's declaration of pregnancy, Ruby was to bear a child, and the name of the child would be . . .

NAMING RIGHTS – THE DILEMMA STARTS

Oh God, we're going to have to name this thing. What on earth do we call our kid? How do we decide? And if we disagree, are the marriage conflict seminars we did good enough to overcome the ongoing dispute? At dinner that night Ruby paused with a spoonful of matso dumpling soup midway between bowl and mouth and said, 'We should call her M for now.' She slurped the thin broth and added, 'I'm allowed to do that, I'm pregnant.'

I didn't believe she was being deliberately incomprehensible, but this was a total mystery. Call *her*? It's definitely a girl? And Emfanow? Empha Now? M4 Now? And 'allowed to do' what – *call* her Emphanow? How now Emfanow? I thought it needed explanation.

'Allowed to do what?'

'Slurp my soup,' she replied with her big cheerful grin. 'There have to be some perks.' Well that was simple.

I went on, 'And her? Are you sure it's going to be a girl?'

'It's going to be a girl,' she said, and patted her flat tummy confidently. 'I'll make you a deal. If I'm right and it's a girl, you have to buy me a full body work-over after the birth – massage, facial, the whole bit – to help me over the trauma. If it's a boy, you don't have to attend the birth, but you can hand around cigars outside afterwards.'

'Well, that's fair,' I replied. 'We might not find out whether it's a boy or a girl until after it's born and besides, I might want to be at the birth.'

'You'd better be,' she said between slurps. 'Is it a deal?'

'Is that one of those perks?' I asked.

'I've got to milk this thing,' she said. 'You can't just feel awful all the time.'

'And why do you want to call it Emfanow?' I inquired.

'Not Emfanow,' she replied, 'M, for now. For the moment.'

'M?' I asked.

'For embryo. We have to refer to it as someone in the meantime, so I thought M, for embryo.'

It stood to reason. Conceived after *Dr No*, M was now in charge, directing the shots and telling us what to do, what to eat, when to sleep, when to feel good and bad, and generally taking control of our lives. For the next nine months, Ruby's womb would be the control room for a hidden secret agent, an unknown operative, subverting our free lifestyles and dictating our behaviour. Our mission, and we could not choose to refuse it, was to get the bugger out in nine months time. Ruby had a licence, to be ill.

'By the way,' I asked, 'Did the doctor say how pregnant you are?'

'Five to six weeks,' she replied between slurps of soup. 'That's taken from when I had my last period, so it's really about four to five weeks since conception. I'm a month gone already.'

A month gone already and we didn't even know. Nights of boozy parties, hard exercise, rich foods, hard exercise, late nights, more hard exercise and all the time something tiny was brewing inside her. Breaking down from one cell to two, to four, to eight, and planting itself on the lining of her uterus while all around the world gurgled, burped and rumbled, as it was jerked about, intoxicated, sweated, slept on, and occasionally squashed by a hundred kilogram lug of future father. Our M. It was now time to take control, M had said, mutely ensconced in the dark folds of its control centre. It had issued its first command.

'I feel disgusting,' said Ruby and, tying her hair back, staggered off to the bathroom.

HOW IT ALL STARTS

A month old already and I realised I had no real idea of what was actually happening inside Ruby's belly. Of course I knew the basics. I went to the sex talks in third grade at school, and learnt that *the* baby is made by inserting *the* penis into *the* vagina, so that when *the* sperm are released they connect with *the* ovum, so *the* foetus can grow in *the* womb. Have no doubt, these classes were the definite article.

I recall I only had two questions after those talks, both of which I was too shy to ask:

- How does the penis get inserted into the vagina when it's such a floppy little thing?

- Is that my recently disappeared Batmobile that the class thief Michael Gibbs is playing with?

I only ever figured out one of these. But now a zillion questions were coming at me. I wanted to know every detail about my child and how it was formed, right from the start. Here's a test of knowledge about the process:

1. How many sperm do we men make in order to conceive a child? Is it:

   a. 1,000 per second (as if!),
   b. 1,000 per day (day trippers), or
   c. 20,000 per 100 millilitres of full strength alcohol beer (that's my boys!).

2. How many eggs does Ruby make in the hope that she might conceive? Is it:

   a. all 5 million of them before she's even born (too weird!),
   b. one a month (**Production Monthly Timetable**), or
   c. one per 100millilitres of full strength alcohol beer (that's my girl!).

They didn't tell us these things in third grade. So I got some books out. There are any number of titles which give you the details from fertilisation to birth. Ones I found useful included:

Every Woman by Dr Derek Llewellyn-Jones, (Faber & Faber, 1989).

A Child is Born (with photographs) by Lennart Nilsson and Lars Hamberger, (Doubleday, 1990). Lennart is the Norwegian medico I mentioned earlier. This book has some truly amazing photography.

I also checked out the BBC's *Human Body* video which was screened by the ABC a while ago and is available in ABC bookshops. The first and second episodes of this had some remarkable statistics and extraordinary photography: it was a bit like the video of Lennart's book.
Taking it from the very beginning this is what happens:

THE SPERM

Our testicles are two incredible sperm production units. They do us proud. A thing called the pituitary gland deep within the brain stem which controls much of our growth and reproduction tells the testicles to produce sperm-making hormones. One of the hormones produced by the testicles is the famous testosterone which, aside from growing our beards each day, helps the sperm and male sex organs mature. In fact, newly-born boys already have immature sperm, but real production does not start until puberty. And, boy, does it take off then.

Inside each testicle there are several hundred metres (yes, you read that correctly) of coiled sperm-making tubes, magnificently named *seminiferous tubules*. Primitive sperm form just beneath the outer edge of these tubules, and over about two months as they mature they move towards a tiny open duct at the centre. When the sperm reach the middle of the tubule, they are fully mature and get transported to a holding tank on an outside part of the testicle called the *epididymis* (although they haven't left the scrotum yet). There they sit, waiting for the call. Probably doing push-ups or something.

The head of each sperm contains a copy of our genetic biomap. It also contains an enzyme to help it penetrate the wall of the egg should it get that far. Behind the head is its little tail which, when swimming, gives it that frenetic tadpole appearance under the electron microscope.

SOME INTERESTING FIGURES

Rate of sperm production: 1,000 per second. (That's right, the answer to question 1 was (a), light speed: every minute of every day, sleeping, eating, jogging, etc. That's 87 million per day, in round figures. That's a thousand copies of us each second.)

Average ejaculation 2-5 millilitres. (I'd like to know who measured theirs to work out the average.)

Sperm per ejaculation 500 million. (Yep, about five day's work, which is probably why we need a break every now and then.)

Size of each sperm Six one-hundredths of a millimetre long. (Give or take a nanometre. Place them end to end and you've got 30 kilometres per load. Yeehah!)

During sex, in fact at the point of ejaculation, sperm are thrust ('at great speed', says Lennart's book, but without a radar check) from the epididymis along a tube called the *vas deferens*. Along the way they are given two lots of energy boosters, the first in chemical form by the prostate gland, and then as seminal fluid from glands called the *seminal vesicles*. Fully charged, they rush into the urethra, along the penis, and then out to begin the hunt for . . .

THE OVUM

Women are different (in case you hadn't noticed). Some say the female reproductive system looks a bit like the Toyota insignia: the central *uterus* with *ovaries* on either side and the *cervix* and the vagina below it. Oh what a feeling.

Women have all their eggs (or *ova* – one *ovum*, two *ova*) in place before they're even born. By the fifth month of gestation, the internal and external sex organs of the female foetus are fully formed, and her tiny foetal ovaries contain all the eggs she will ever produce in her life. Again, the answer to question 2 was (a), which, I say again, is too weird. Before a baby girl is born, she holds about five million possibilities for the future within her. Not that she'll use them all. During her fertile years she will release only about 400 of these, once a month.

When I say released, that's exactly what happens. The ova are contained in the ovaries in little capsules known as *follicles*. At ovulation, the pituitary gland (we've seen that one before) sends hormones into the bloodstream instructing the ovaries to produce the female hormone oestrogen. This stimulates the release of the follicle into the *fallopian tube*. On average, one ovum is released by one ovary each month. Why they take turns is anyone's guess, but I suppose it's nature's way of ensuring that if one ovary is lost, the other can do the job on a monthly basis.

The released ovum is drawn into the fallopian tube by feather-like hairs, or *fimbriae*, on the wall of the fallopian tube where it ruptures, exposing the ovum. The ovum waits for a sperm to come along, leaning seductively against the wall of the fallopian tube. Hi boys. Meanwhile, the lining of the uterus (called the *endometrium*) gets thicker, to nurture the fertilised egg if fertilisation takes place. In the absence of fertilisation, the egg lasts for a few days before it exits the uterus along with the thickened endometrium, giving rise to the cycle of bleeding known as *menstruation*, or having a period.

But, if she misses her period, then you have . . .

FERTILISATION

It's true: the beginning of a child – the beginning of you and me – is a fascinating story. It's a tale of incredible odds, of chance, adventure and violence, of nurture and survival, of a creature inhabiting new worlds and a universe synchronised for its benefit.

The sperm's journey has five stages once it leaves the penis:

the *vagina* which they enter first. From there into . . .

the *cervix* (the tube connecting the vagina to the uterus). Then into . . .

the *uterus* (also known as the womb). And up into . . .

the *fallopian tubes* (which connect the uterus to the ovaries) to hunt out . . .

the *ovum* which lies in waiting. That is, the egg isn't fertilised in the womb, but in the fallopian tube.

The sperm's journey is about fifteen to eighteen centimetres from vagina to egg. At 1/600 millimetres in length, it's about the equivalent of a grown adult swimming from Melbourne to Perth, in total darkness, along with ten per cent of the world's population and using only instinct as a guide. Some sperm do it in about half an hour. Others take hours or days. Most don't even get close.

This is because almost immediately the sperm leave the penis, 400 million are slaughtered by the natural acidity of the vagina. Bummer. Only those that can escape into a protective mucus produced by the cervix can avoid the massacre. Even then they have to dodge the bombardment of the woman's white blood cells, the main armoury in her immune system which kills everything foreign to her body. And sperm are foreigners. Teensy bits of men in a hostile female sea, like swimmers dodging great white sharks in a dark forbidding ocean.

Many get lost in the numerous folds in the cervix. Others choose the wrong fallopian tube. Some die. Some are poisoned. Some are killed. In fact, only about 1,000 make it anywhere near the egg. And even then, they can swim right past it.

For the very few who actually get to the egg, the race has just begun. Fierce competitors, they attack the hard outer crust of the egg with all their instinctive strength. Their heads frenetically hammer against the hard surface, and they drill in with all the energy their spiralling tails can muster. They shed the cap on their heads and release the enzymes I mentioned before, to burn through the ovum's outer layer. Basically, they head butt it like crazy, then spit at it. This is assault. Competition at its most violent.

Suddenly, one sperm breaks through the wall – victory! The winner! Immediately satisfied, the ovum slams the gate shut on every other loser dangling outside, by mutating her chemical composition. She's scored her man, and no-one's going to intrude. Some of the losers will hang around her for days to come. She doesn't care. They'll die. She has the one she wants. Her knight in white liquid.

Meanwhile, the winner can relax. There's no competition now, only the inevitable fusion of two halves of a future person. He's discarded his tail and cruises towards the central nucleus of the ovum which holds the woman's genetic material as its secret treasure and final goal. Inextricably drawn together, the male and the female nuclei touch and fuse.

In this instant, the miracle of creation occurs, as a whole new potential is born, entirely itself, derived from mother and father, a future yet to be realised.

In this instant, the hereditary characteristics of a new individual are created. All its physiology, its eye colour, its height, its predisposition to heart failure, how big its feet will be, whether it will go bald, the likelihood of inherited diseases, its body shape, hairy buttocks, knock knees, buck teeth, everything from mother and father. Everything, in the flash of nucleic fusion.

The mother holds a fertilised egg within her.

After that, the new thing has to become . . . the *embryo*.

What's happening to it

Month One About 2–6 mm. Thickness of a coin.

The journey of the fertilisers might be finished, but not the journey of the fertilised. The first month of the embryo's life sees an extraordinary number of changes. Roughly speaking it goes like this:

Fertilisation One cell with complete genetic material. The DNA has been established for the future child.

12 hours Two cells appear after division of the first single cell. Each cell divides again about every half day.

2 days Four to eight cells, still in the fallopian tube, heading towards the uterus.

4 to 5 days The cluster of about 100 cells is now called a *blastocyst* and the aim is to attach itself to the uterus, usually the ceiling, on the endometrium. It tumbles along the uterus until its outer skin breaks and it settles into its chosen spot. At this point the cells begin to differentiate, becoming half *placenta* and half embryo. The placenta is the embryo's food pack for the next nine months. Some fertilised eggs don't make it to the uterus but get caught in the fallopian tubes, resulting in an *ectopic pregnancy*. This can be fatal to the mother if not removed.

8 to 10 days The blastocyst has secured its position on the ceiling of the uterus by anchor ropes called *trophoblasts*. Progesterone is secreted by the ovary back to the pituitary gland to say menstruation is not needed any more. The Eagle has landed. A mucous plug cements the cervix closed so nothing can escape the brewing chamber of the uterus. There are now about 200 cells. Commence Program Growth. Miraculously, cells in the blastocyst prevent the mother's immune system from killing it, which should happen because the blastocyst, like the sperm it came from, is a foreign body made up partially from the father.

12 days Now a couple of million cells. The trophoblasts develop into the *amniotic sac*, the bag of fluid in which the embryo will grow, and the *umbilical cord*.

2 weeks About 2 millimetres long. The embryo looks like a speck of dust. It has three different layers of cells which begin to differentiate into different types of body parts. The outer layer turns into parts such as the brain, spine and nervous system. The middle layer creates the inner layers of skin, bones and muscles including the heart, blood cells, reproductive components and kidneys. The inner layer gives rise to such things as the lungs and urinary tract. Under a microscope the whole thing looks kind of like a sea slug.

1 month By one month the embryo is clearly distinguishable, being about 6 millimetres long with a tiny beating heart, the beginnings of a brain, a suggestion of where the spine might be and the beginning of lungs. It's tied by the umbilical cord to the placenta at the point that will become its belly button, below which is a tail. It looks a bit like a baby witchetty grub with small fish gills. These gills develop into the mouth and jaw, neck and face but it doesn't look anything like a baby just yet.

The embryo floats inside the amniotic sac, connected by the umbilical cord to the placenta. The placenta is the organ which gathers nutrients from the mother, which it exchanges for the foetal waste which is disbursed through the mother's system.

THE WHOLE KIT IS A BIT LIKE THIS

Length: About 2–6 mm.

Brain: Very rudimentary at this stage. Growing at 100 million cells every minute. By birth it will be about 100 billion cells. Eighteen years later, only 55 will be left after the football season ends.

Heart: Developed early to feed the rest of the embryo.

Backbone: Very rudimentary. Like a prawn back. Forty *somites*, blocks of bone, eight of which are the tail which will disappear.

Eyes: Just a crater in the forehead. The nerve stalk from the brain reaches to the skin and the forehead. The end of the skin thickens to become the future eyeball.

Ears: A hollow in the side of the head is the future inner ear. It is joined by initial cells from the pharynx to form the foundations of the hammer, anvil and stirrup.

Limbs: A stripe on the side of the embryo extends from the future shoulders to the future hips, as if marking the place for them.

Sex Gender is determined at the moment of fertilisation, but the sexual organs are not able to be seen until about two months (if you actually took the embryo out and examined it), and gender is not fully obvious on an ultrasound until about four months.

It looks a bit like a very small, but living, trilobite. Or a gumby. At one month, this was our M.

What's happening to her

This section of each chapter is meant to be only a general guide to the process from the mother's side of the deal. It's not meant to be a definitive guide to what happens, physically, medically, or emotionally, to the mother-to-be. There's no way I could cover that. I'm not a doctor or a psychologist, and it would be impossible to describe the entire range of experiences that your wife or partner will have. Go to the other books I mentioned earlier on for that kind of detail.

What you'll read here is a summary of *some* of what will go on, and what you will have to assist her with. Not a complete list, just some of the most common things. Use it as a kind of starting point if you want, as an introduction to what she might be going through, and a springboard for discussion of her experiences and how you can help (or get in the way as the case may be). For example, if you ask her whether she is experiencing some of the things on the list, don't feel that something is wrong if she's not. It's just that what's happening to her is different from the summary. The thing about this pregnancy business is that everyone has an opinion, from your old auntie to the green grocer in the local corner shop. As a result, there's a lot of guilt flying around, and a lot of people who'll fuel feelings of doubt and concern. Someone will say, 'Ooh, you aren't very big.' The next will say the opposite, 'You're huge!' Someone will say, 'Ooh, you can't eat that!' The next will say the opposite, 'That's a great source of iron, you should eat it.' And so on.

Take it all with a grain of salt. By all means listen to them, patiently, but follow your intuition and that of your wife or partner. The trouble is that the whole thing is so new, it's hard to trust your instincts. She has no past history to go by, we men have even less, and she has a whole range of new things happening to her body that have never occurred to her before. You can go to the books for more detail, and more importantly, to your doctor. Ultimately it's the GP, *obstetrician* and professional *midwife* who can answer the questions you need answered. Check with them about any problems you have and issues you need to discuss. If you have doubts, get a second opinion. There's an extraordinary variety of approaches to pregnancy and birth. Some people insist on having an obstetrician, others insist on midwives only. Some obstetricians and midwives are very laidback in their views, others take an interventionist approach, some support natural birthing, others insist upon going to hospital. Some promote vaginal delivery, some will advise *caesars*, some early *epidurals* and so on. At the end of the day, they are the professionals (people with insurance) and specialists (people with loads of study in the area) who know the most about what's going on inside the mother's body. Despite all the criticism of obstetricians (and associated lawsuits and insurance issues) they will have a major role to play in navigating your way through pregnancy and labour, especially if complications arise.

Well, that's enough opinionating from me. What's happening to her? First up, there are signs she's pregnant. These include:

No period.
This is the real give away, especially if your partner's periods are regular. However, there may be other reasons, so it's time to get a pregnancy test kit. And then, some women continue with some form of spotting the whole way through. She might tell you that, she might not.

A positive result on the test kit.
This may be two blue lines, a red line, or however the test kit works. Another real give away. But then again, the tests are only 99 per cent accurate. Also, it may be too early to take it. It has to be taken after her next period is due, or it will be too early to get a positive result. If in doubt, ask your doctor.

Morning sickness.
Nausea and vomiting can be caused by anything from bad prawns to the Ebola virus, but combined with no menstruation and a positive test result, it's a fairly good indicator of what's to come.

Her breasts start getting bigger.
They are preparing to become mammaries. This usually goes with the darkening of the nipples (the *areolae*).

Tiredness.
It's almost guaranteed she will start wanting sleep, sleep, and more sleep.

The first three months – the first trimester – is generally the worst. It's also the trickiest for the embryo/foetus. All the essential foundations of your future child are being laid down, such as heart, lungs and other vital organs, genetic replication, the brain and limbs. It's a time when things are most likely to go wrong. It's also the time when the mother needs to take most care about her own health, to safeguard the health of your baby.

For this reason, read the books about:

Foods she should and shouldn't eat (Is it okay to eat smoked sausage, crustaceans, sushi, and soft cheeses? How about fruit and other nice things?);

The effects of drugs (Can she take panadol, caffeine or vitamin supplements? Can she drink alcohol, assuming she can stand the taste? How about cigarettes, ecstasy, marijuana and other fun things?);

Illnesses she should know about (What's hypothermia, listeriosis, rubella? What's the effect of STDs, AIDS, vaginal bleeding and other scary things?);

Environments to avoid (What happens if she gets sunburnt, needs an x-ray, sprays bugs with pesticides and other nasty things?); and

Safe activities (Is it okay to go bungee-jumping, jogging, high altitude skiing, surfing or partying? Can she still have sex and other pleasant things?).

This is not a definitive list of do's and don'ts; it's just a way to get the ball rolling. Make a joint list of questions for the obstetrician or midwife to answer. In fact, visits to the obstetrician can be fun. They reveal the first positive indications of life inside the womb. Up until now, the only signs you will have had are a positive test kit result, verified by a urine sample at your local doctor, and a bunch of adverse physical symptoms like morning sickness. The obstetrician will probably test for the heartbeat – and when it appears your own heart will leap in your chest. There's something alive in there! You might even get a preliminary ultrasound too, to determine the size of the foetus, and hence its age.

Anyway, roll on Month Two. We had a half-baked gumby the size of a gnat for a daughter (if it is a daughter), a nauseous soup-slurping mother and a father brain dead with delirium – the good, the bad and the ugly. Situation normal, apparently.

Coming to terms

What's happening to me

IN THE FAMILY WAY

In keeping with our agreement, I told my parents, my sister and two very close friends that week. Not in keeping with our agreement, I also told six other friends, four work colleagues, three total strangers, the barber, the butcher and our travel agent (well, I had to cancel our airline tickets).

Dad was the first to hear the news. He'd never been a talker when it came to the phone. Typically, when I rang he'd say, 'Hello, old boy. Just hang on and I'll get your mother.' If I had something important to announce, (for example, a new lawn mower or a career change) he'd tell me just how I felt because he, like all of us men, had been through it, and I was just about to learn about it. Then he would get my mother.

So, when I told him Ruby was pregnant, he said, 'Pregnant! That's great news, old boy. I'm very happy for you.' I waited. 'I know just what you're going through,' he said. 'That feeling of general happiness. Like all men, I've been through it too. You're about to see life from the other side of the fence. The best thing you can do is give her everything she wants. Hang on, I'll get your mother.'

My mother, on the other hand, is always happy to chat on the phone, provided she's comfortably installed with a cup of tea. Her voice skipped across the cables, 'What's this? What's this news?' I was about to reply when she said, 'Hang on, I'll just get myself settled. I was just having a cup of tea.' I heard her take a sip. 'Aaah, that's better, now what's this news?'

I could see the smile spread across her face as we spoke and felt her immediate pride at becoming a grandmother for the first time. I'd never suspected my parents of being sentimental about having grandchildren. They'd never pressured me to have any, but it was evident from that moment on that they were thrilled. I had to explain everything I knew about M from her time of conception (no graphic detail, of course), to her state of development, her current and future potential names (none at this stage), to Ruby's health ('No, I can't put her on, Mum, it's Monday. I'm at work').

Then the strangest thing happened. She began to tell me of her birth experiences: how many hours labour she went through with my sister (seven, it seems), then me (five) – so short labours. My mother didn't so much eschew pain as tell it to piss off while she got on with whatever job was at hand. She told me how she used to sit on the edge of the bed before I was born, naked in the summer heat, and wonder how this thing was going to come out of her. (This thing, indeed!) She told me that my sister came out face down. She told me in detail about the surgery she needed after I was born ('Not that I minded, I was under a general anaesthetic').

At first I thought this isn't the kind of thing a son wants to hear from his mother. But then I thought, hang on, Mum's sharing something deep here. Childbirth is a fundamental thing for her, and she's letting me in on the secrets of it, because I was about to embark on the process myself, sort of. It was as if a part of my life was now being authenticated in my parents' eyes. By rite of passage I was now entitled to hear their experiences of life and its progeny.

Ruby told her parents that night and I could hear the screams of delight echoing down the phone line. Ten minutes after they'd hung up, the phone rang and when I answered it Grandmaruby was on the line: 'I thought I should congratulate the father,' she exclaimed. 'After all, you have a part to play in all this too. We shouldn't forget that fathers are involved. It's not just the woman's thing.'

What could I say? Wise words indeed. I am to be involved in this process. Just how, I was still finding out, because obviously I was not the one actually doing the growth work. There were no hormones flushing around in my system, making me tired, irritable, nauseous or fixated on matso dumpling soup. However, I was sure I would have an active role to play in the pregnancy, the birth (if I could stomach it) and afterwards.

I also thought that it was good to have the grandparents on side. You can't be selfish in times like these, but let's face facts. All my friends who have children say that grandparents are the happiest babysitters, and therefore the best source of allowing you the freedom to go out at night. I'd always wondered whether my own parents would be the type to pat the baby with a grimace like an unwanted lap dog and then hand it back saying, 'Here, it's yours to look after. Now clean its bottom.' But no, they were as hooked as me.

GOING PUBLIC

All my male friends praised the pregnancy as my own stunning achievement. They pumped my hand and exclaimed, 'Congratulations! Well done!' as if I'd done a wonderful thing (which when I thought about it, I *had* done). On one occasion I tried to play down the importance of my role. 'All I did was have sex, on some unspecified night, which resulted in a pregnancy.' But they were resolute. 'No, they're your swimmers, mate. They got through. Welcome to the Club.'

The Club. The select band (of how many millions?) of men who've got a woman up the duff. Our badge of honour. Our source of pride, that one of our sperm had struck home. No mistake, I had infiltrated the mysteries of womanhood, and had staked my claim on her deepest held secrets. It was as if this intent – fertilisation – drove every ejaculation. Every time we come we secretly want to seed.

One of the two chosen friends, Guru Dave, had some of his usual words of wisdom. He pointed out how animal the process can be. 'Her body takes over, and she has no control over it,' he said. 'She gets bigger, she gets told what to eat, to slow down, when to move, when to rest. And it doesn't stop at the birth, either. It goes on. Her body just makes milk, and the milk changes according to how old the baby is. We think we have rational minds and free will, but it's like a preordained system, it just steams ahead. You can't control it. It overtakes you. It's really animal.' Frightening. Good-bye Ruby, I thought. See you when we're old and it's all over.

His other remark set me thinking. 'You're getting through your life goals,' he said. I hadn't thought of it that way. Marriage and fatherhood were the two life goals he was referring to, but I'd never called them that. From very early on, Ruby and I had agreed we wanted to have children, and it happened pretty quickly. We had our first date two months after we met, I proposed three weeks after that, we were married nine months later, and then, five months after that, she was pregnant.

You could be forgiven for thinking that a biological clock had sounded an alarm, it was so quick. Normally we only speak of women having a biological clock – meaning they want to bear children before they get too old. There might be five million eggs in storage inside them, but only a select few are released. Once they reach about forty years old, things start to slow down, both in the release of eggs and the ability of the body to cope with the trauma of bearing a child. The risk of abnormalities significantly increases the older they get. When you think about it, our bodies were fashioned in the ancient wilds of Africa, and we became parents as soon as we went through puberty. Nowadays we're having children at an age when, in evolutionary terms, we're actually old enough to be grandparents. Basically Ruby, who was approaching thirty-five, wanted to beat the clock, and I was more than happy to stop the alarm.

The question is, do men also have a biological clock? We don't have the same age limit on sperm production, and can manufacture the little fellas well into old age. (At 1,000 per second over 70 years, that's a total of – oh forget it). There are plenty of really old dads around, especially those who married young a second time. To my mind, that was where the biological clock issue arose. If you have kids too late in life, you risk the possibility that you'll lack the energy to be involved in bringing them up. You'll be old when they're teenagers, which, my older friends tell me, is the time when you need all your powers of strength and patience. I wanted to be sure I had time enough to enjoy their energy. It may not be as strong as a woman's biological clock, because we can at least have kids into our fifties and beyond, but it was still an issue to be considered. I was grateful to Ruby for helping me out. All of which sounds a bit unromantic, but hey, I didn't say we weren't having a hoot doing it.

The other question was, what are my life goals? What other ambitions were lurking deep inside my subconscious? In my late thirties, should I not be able to list them, along with an action plan about how to achieve them? There are plenty of magazines which regularly list the things we ought to have done by the time we're thirty, most involving sex (threesomes, mile-high club etc.), but what about real life? Or to put it another way, when my kids are thirty and I ask them to express in ten words or less what I taught them, what do I want them to say?

own a house?
be the boss by the time I'm 50?
retire at 55?
be worth $60 million by 60?
join the mile high club by the time I'm 30?
climb Everest?
move to the country?
live overseas?
find God?
give him back?
make the world a better place?
etc . . . ?

Or does all that place too many restrictions on life: closing doors to unexpected experiences in deference to an established list of goals? What if you get to the end and realise you didn't want the goals you set? What if they change halfway through life? Right now it seemed they had. The one certain thing was that M's arrival in seven and a half months time would radically alter whatever goals I might've had. Whatever I did from now on would have to accommodate the baby, in fact accommodate the whole family: M, Ruby and me. Some goals, like threesomes, would be totally off the list. Others, like climbing Everest would be severely delayed, and others like holding down a remunerative job, would take on greater priority. I'm not saying these were my particular goals, but you know what I mean . . . The main goal for the next twenty years at least, was to be a good parent, (whatever that meant). I had some basic ideas at this early stage, but I decided to go with the concept that whatever constitutes being a good parent would only become clear when M arrived. I could have the best intentions and read all the best books, but until M came into the world I wouldn't know what she(he) might find helpful and beneficial. So I just drew up a list of foundation principles which I thought might be a useful starting point:

love;
respect;
care;
opportunity;
happiness;
passion;
peace;
self knowledge.

If I could instil these things in M I figured I would be off to a good start. I also figured if I could instil these things in myself I'd be off to a good middle (as in middle age).

The other good friend I told about the pregnancy was Stu, aka Single Stu. I'd phoned him with the news, and we fixed a time to go out and celebrate. Ruby had to fly to Korea for work for a few days, so I took the opportunity to hook up with him for dinner at an inner city pub. Unlike the wise parent Guru Dave, Single Stu is very single, and is in fact one of Sydney's most eligible but unknown bachelors: great fun, generous, warm-hearted and a loyal friend. It was he who introduced Ruby to me eighteen months ago. Seated at a balcony table high among the emerald leaves of the trees that graced the cobbled lanes, we feasted on fresh bread, steak and beer. We toasted M, Ruby, his various loves, our trip overseas last year, and as the beers took hold, we watched the evening fade from dusk to dark and the yellow street lights emerge from the red bougainvillea and ivy-clad walls below.

I decided, this is what pregnancy is all about. Sitting on a pub verandah having a beer or four with your mates, mopping up the gravy with a hunk of bread, and finally leaning back in your chair to contemplate the glory of life. You've kicked a (life) goal, son. Have one for the road.

I learned later it was about this time that Ruby was trying not to vomit for the umpteenth time at the sight of the umpteenth plate of raw jelly fish at the umpteenth banquet in Korea. I met her at the airport with a dozen red roses. An ashen grimace greeted me from behind a mountain of luggage.

TEMPER TIME

'God I feel disgusting,' she said. 'I've had five days of not eating raw jellyfish, not drinking wine, and not eating anything except chilli cabbage. My breasts hurt, my stomach is nauseous, the flight was horrendous because I couldn't sit still, takeoff and landing sent me spinning into a vomit, I haven't slept, I'm jetlagged, I'm hot, I'm sweaty and I need a shower. It's good to see you.'

I took hold of the luggage trolley and gave her the roses. She pressed her nose into the red petals and breathed in deeply.

'Do these have a perfume?' she asked. 'My sense of smell has gone.' She dumped them unceremoniously on top of the luggage. When I gave her a welcome home kiss, she grimaced, 'Yuck, you taste revolting.' I'd cleaned my teeth especially well in anticipation of a warm welcome home smooch.

'Metallic,' she explained. 'My taste buds have gone too. It's nothing you've done wrong.' Done wrong? I thought. Was she on the lookout for things I might've done wrong? I book-marked the thought for future reference. Pushing the loaded trolley into the car park I offered comfortingly, 'I've stocked up on matso dumpling soup, so you won't starve.'

'Can't stand the stuff,' she replied. 'Can we have some cheese and tomato on toast?' Luckily I'd stocked the Ruby pantry to cater for all pregnancy contingencies, but she added, 'I'll just get a bag of Twisties for now.'

Well, maybe not all contingencies.

'I thought you said they had too much MSG,' I grunted, heaving suitcases into the boot of the car. I watched the car sink a bit. I could've sworn she didn't have so many bags when she left.

'They do,' she replied. 'But I just want them.'

'I thought you said you had to be careful about what you eat in case it affects M,' I said hoisting another case in and checking the level of the car.

'After the way the little bugger's been treating me lately I don't care what she gets,' came her solemn reply.

'You aren't worried it might make you feel worse?'

'I can give as good as I get,' she replied. I wondered whether this was the basis for a healthy mother/daughter(son) relationship so I tried to put a more positive spin on it.

'Is there a placenta now to regulate all that? Do we have a placenta yet?' But she ignored the question. 'You didn't bring Tiger to meet me.'

No, I didn't think the airport staff would have appreciated an exuberant dog upsetting throngs of anxious relatives waiting for jetlagged loved ones. Clearly, though, from Ruby's expression I should have disregarded all that and brought the dog. When we arrived home, Tiger threw herself at Ruby in a fit of ecstasy, and Ruby responded in kind, burying her head in a flurry of golden fur and juggling limbs. 'Tiger!' she screamed delightedly as Tiger licked her face. 'I missed you, my darling!'

What had I done wrong? Perhaps if I hadn't bought roses and had gargled with dog saliva I might have had a warmer reception. I was just lugging the first of the bags from the car, when I heard a scream from inside the house.

'What's happened?' I called anxiously. Cramps I thought? Bleeding? Miscarriage? My mind raced from disaster to tragedy, and I rushed into the house to investigate. By the time I arrived she was standing at the bathroom door looking very distressed.

'This bathroom is disgusting!' she declared. 'What have you been doing in here?' I stared at the bathroom. White tiles stared back at me with inscrutable blankness. I could see nothing wrong. The toilet was clean, the basin glistened, the bath and shower disclosed not a single deficiency.

'It's filthy,' she exclaimed. I looked again at the same white walls, the clear glass shower screen, the shiny chrome taps. I was at a complete loss. Were

I decided, this is what pregnancy is all about. Sitting on a pub verandah having a beer or four with your mates, mopping up the gravy with a hunk of bread, and finally leaning back in your chair to contemplate the glory of life. You've kicked a (life) goal, son. Have one for the road.

the towels not evenly folded, or the legions of shampoo and toiletries not properly ordered? Perhaps the soap dish needed a second cake of soap. Whatever it was, it eluded me.

'What's wrong with it?' I asked, and immediately knew I shouldn't have.

'It's filthy,' she repeated. 'Look, there's dust everywhere. Lint from the towels, dog hair, there look,' and she pointed at the spotless terrain of bathroom tiles below me. 'And up there,' pointing at the top of the clean shower screen, and there, and there, and . . .

'You've been splashing again,' she said.

Splashing? I thought, from the shower? Is that a hanging offence in Korea nowadays?

'Every time you men go to the toilet you shake it everywhere. Why you can't get it in the bowl is beyond me. Why don't you sit down? It smells like a pigsty in here.'

As every man knows, we don't miss. We aim for the bowl, we get the bowl, we shake in the bowl and we leave the space as fragrant as we found it. Yet half the world's population seems to think we go to the bathroom with malicious intent to mark our territory in every possible place *except* the toilet. This difference will never be resolved but was clearly aggravating Ruby's temper at the moment. Besides, I thought she said she'd lost her sense of smell.

'It's more acute,' she said. 'I can pick out the bad things.'

I thought of the child-catcher in *Chitty Chitty Bang Bang*.

'And look at this!' she said. 'Pubic hairs. They're all over the place.' Not that I could see them, but I looked anyway, straining my eyes for the tell-tale signs of curly black on white. They must have straightened themselves out and hidden in the grout between the tiles. I didn't think it prudent to ask her to pick one out for me, but foolishly I couldn't resist stirring the pot. I didn't realise how serious things could get.

'It might not be pubic,' I said. 'It might be a chest hair, leg hair, arm hair or even a bum hair.'

She whipped around venomously. 'Whatever it is, it's your hair and it's all over the place. I've been away five days and you haven't lifted a bloody finger. Men are disgusting!'

'May I remind you,' I reminded her, 'that this particular disgusting man is the father of the child you're carrying.'

'Well you'd better shape up then,' she yelled as she closed the door in my face.

'It's my baby too!' I never thought I'd hear myself utter those words, and even though I was joking, I was surprised by a core of meaning. My surprise was short-lived, as she bellowed through the door, 'Don't bet on it!'.

That was low, very low. I'd been prepared for moody bouts on regular battle fields, even clichéd areas like bathroom hygiene, but this was a different ball game. Usually spoken in jest, these words now carried a nefarious ring of truth about them which was aimed to hurt. It attacked the essential trust of parenthood. It withheld what should be most intimately shared. It disowned me. I was collateral, irrelevant and abused. I had a sudden rush of anger and fear. Anger at the injustice of her remark and unanticipated fear of its possibility. At this stage in fatherhood, we have no real way of knowing whether we actually are parents. DNA tests can prove the matter after the birth, but this requires at least eight months more waiting. And the unfairness of forcing this fear into my mind left me seething.

I opened the door and looked at Ruby slouched beneath the jets of water. It took all my might not to re-enact the shower scene from *Psycho*. Instead, I asked through taut lips, 'Is this a pregnant mood thing, or jet lag, or just everything?' She looked at me tearfully for a long moment as the water poured over her and steam filled the room. Then she said, 'I can't stop it. I missed you in Korea. It was really silly because I was only away five days, and I'm always so independent. But I just wanted to be with you and have you look after me. I wanted you there and you weren't.'

'Welcome home,' I said, and kissed her lightly on the lips, avoiding the possibility of metallic feedback. 'I'll make you some cheese and tomato on toast.'

PRESENTS FOR AN IMPENDING DAD

When she was dressed, Ruby emptied the mountains of bags over the living room floor and pulled out vast numbers of presents and souvenirs for family and friends. Tea-sets, teapots, wall hangings, woven decorations of bright blue, red and yellow materials, magazines, travel brochures and loads of duty free alcohol, chocolate and cosmetics.

'Friends' shopping lists,' she explained.

Last to emerge was a vacuum-sealed ceramic bottle of Korean rice wine. I looked at it, trying to disguise revulsion with gratitude as my sense of smell recoiled in horror. The bulbous pot was harmless enough, but its stink was evil. Somehow the aroma had escaped the vacuum-sealed plastic, gagging my nose and mouth, shrivelling my tongue and making the hairs on the back of my neck not just stand up, but jump off and run away. It was the type of stuff that made straight metho smell like cordial. Tiger fled the house, her tail between her legs.

'I bought this for you,' Ruby said proudly as she thrust the brown bottle in its revolting fog towards me. 'Only you'll have to drink it all, because I can't drink.' I held it delicately in both hands, like I was holding a bomb which might explode any minute. My eyes began to water, and I fully expected my fingers to start burning as though they'd been dipped in an acid bath. 'Do you like it?' she asked. I couldn't lie, so I dodged.

'Can you smell it?' I asked.

'Nope,' she replied. 'Is it strong?'

'Is it strong! Week old road-kill smells like perfume compared to this,' I replied. 'Thank you very much for the thought, darling, but I think I'll take it outside'.

'Well, the sniffer dogs didn't pick it up,' she laughed. As I deposited the bottle in the rear courtyard, I had a vision of airport Labradors lying unconscious on the tarmac as airport staff puzzled over their sudden collapse. Tiger snuck back into the house.

Ruby reached in to her handbag and said, 'I bought you this too.' She extracted a narrow white plastic object about six inches long with a rounded end. Its shiny white plastic skin caught the light. I looked at it in wonder. Almost all my friends with children had warned me about the massive reduction in their sex lives but none of them had mentioned this. Surely Ruby was pulling my leg. But apparently she wasn't. Was I supposed to use this on her or me?

'You'll need it for when the baby's born,' she said, as her fingers played gently along its shiny white surface. I was incredulous. *I'll* need it? What for? I couldn't even begin to imagine. She thrust it towards me.

'I got it duty free,' she said. She got it where? Not at any of the duty free shops I'd been to. Was this a Korean speciality? When I took it in my hand it was light and smooth.

'Smell it,' she said. Smell it? It has a fragrance? But I did as she requested, and a mixture of relief and embarrassment swept through me as I inhaled the rich aroma of tobacco from inside the plastic casement. A cigar. Something I'll need when the baby is born. Bought at duty free, with a smell. A cigar.

'I can just see you smoking that,' she said proudly. 'Puffing away with all your mates as a new dad.' I thought this was very strange as I've never smoked a cigar in my life and the last time I tried a cigarette was when I was twenty-one. Smoking always seemed to me like swallowing razor blades.

However, images obviously pop up in the pregnant mind, so I didn't bother to dispel it. And to tell the truth, it kind of appealed to me. I was chuffed that she was taking pride in my future role as father.

Over the next few weeks, Ruby informed me that she'd told all ten of her travelling companions in Korea that she was pregnant. 'I had to. They were all suspicious because I wasn't eating or drinking anything. And you know me, I'm normally a real pisspot.' She'd also told all her work colleagues, a dozen of her closest friends, her hairdresser, her dentist and our architect. 'I told him he now had a deadline,' she said. 'I told him we want to be back in by July so we can have the baby here.'

'You mean have the baby in hospital and then bring it back to the newly renovated house.'

'Yes.'

'That means two things.'

'Yes.'

'Having a baby –'

'Yes.'

'– and renovating the house.'

'Yes.'

'Are you sure you can do both?'

'Yes.'

'Are you feeling sick?'

'Yes.'

'Can you say anything besides yes?'

'Yes.'

A house *and* a baby. We'd planned to renovate some time anyway, but we hadn't planned precisely when. And we certainly hadn't planned to do it now. Similarly we'd planned to have kids, but we hadn't planned precisely when. And we certainly hadn't planned to do it now. In fact we'd put these on hold until after Nepal. It seemed life had got the jump on us.

So while Ruby phoned the architect, I started thinking about having the baby. Not the division of labour I'd expected, but it dawned on me when Ruby mentioned the architect that we were actually going to have a baby. In a short period of time – seven months (the blinking of an eye really) – I would be holding a baby in my arms. My baby. A bundle of pink helplessness wrapped in cotton, resting on my forearm.

NOT HAPPY

The thought knocked me sideways. Suddenly all the happiness I'd experienced over the last month evaporated. The feeling of bliss just disappeared. The realisation that I was going to be responsible for a baby wiped the smile off my face.

But why? Having a baby was what made me so happy in the first place. And now suddenly I wasn't so happy about it. I didn't want to admit it, but it was true – I was suddenly not happy about Ruby being pregnant. And all through a chance remark about an architect. This was really difficult to understand, and took me a couple of weeks to sort through.

Why wasn't I happy? Because I'd lose the privileges of a childless life? We wouldn't be able to go out so easily. We wouldn't be able to meet spontaneously after work for a dinner and movie. We wouldn't be able to go on Nepalese trekking holidays. We wouldn't be able to just go away for a weekend, have friends around for dinner on the spur of the moment, nip down to the pub for a drink, have sex on the couch, go to a party, drink too much and sleep it off in the morning, go bushwalking, jogging, sailing, abseiling, cycling, to the theatre, evening classes, whatever. We just couldn't. Oh sure, we'd learn how to squeeze a few of them in, but not many, and all my friends with kids say you're too tired to do anything at the end of the day anyway. Having a baby means you can't do all that stuff any more. We'd have to knuckle down and raise a rug rat instead.

So I wasn't happy about Ruby being pregnant. And there was something else that I couldn't put my finger on. I wasn't feeling happy, but nor was I angry, or afraid. I didn't have any ill feeling towards Ruby. I didn't blame her for being pregnant (after all, it was half my fault!). I wasn't sad, or lonely or frustrated. I just couldn't figure it out. I spent a fortnight wandering around the house mulling it over. Even Ruby remarked. 'You okay?' I didn't want to tell her I wasn't happy about the pregnancy so I gave her the standard, 'Yeah, fine.'

'You seem upset,' she said.

'No, I'm fine.'

'Sure?'

'Yeah. Fine.' Fine. I probably should've discussed it with her, but I didn't. I figured I might upset her. I felt she needed my support, not my doubts, so I didn't want to tell her what was on my mind until I'd figured out exactly what it was. People tell me that's the difference between men and women: men don't talk until they've worked it all out first, whereas women work it out by talking. Men speak in terms of resolutions, women in terms of questions. Whatever. I'm a man, so I didn't tell her and I struggled on alone to figure out what it was.

Then I realised it was something I should talk to Guru Dave about.

'Dave,' I explained, 'I'm not happy about Ruby being pregnant'. I told him my worries about less time for myself, less time for each other, less flexibility, not having a life and so on.

'Are you happy about being a father?' he asked.

'Oh yeah, that's great.'

'So what's the problem?' Clearly I was missing something. Probably something very simple.

'On the one hand,' he continued, 'you're happy. On the other hand you're not.'

'So what am I then?'

'Both.'

'Both? How can I be both?'

'You're in transition,' he responded.

Ah, transition.

'What the hell is that?'

He enlightened me. 'You're becoming a father. Your life is changing. That's okay. You're about to lose all the benefits of not having kids, which upsets you. That's okay. That's all you've known for nearly 40 years. Going out when you want to. Staying in when you want, all the stuff you mentioned. Of course, you'll miss it. That's okay. Miss it now, so you don't get upset later on. But what you're happy about, and probably really happy about, is becoming a father. You're taking on your new life. You have a new role. And that's good. You haven't done it before – it's a new thing. But you want it. It's what you want, and that's good. Did Ruby mention architects, by the way?'

'Yes, she did. Is that relevant?'

'I don't know,' he said, 'I'm still trying to work it out. My wife did the same thing when she was pregnant. I think it just goes with the territory.'

He was right, as usual. Not about the architect, but about being happy. It wasn't that I wasn't happy. It was that I was happier than I thought I was, which was why I couldn't figure it out. It was a reality check. I'd be holding a baby – my baby – in seven or so months. And that made me really happy. Really deep down inside yabba-dabba-doo happy. I could forget sleep-ins, forget the late night cinema, forget all the other stuff: it was already in the past. There was a shift in my thinking. I was going to be a dad. Deep down, everything else paled into insignificance.

One result of this shift was an improved focus on the tasks at hand. I began thinking more about what M's needs might be, and Ruby's needs and my own needs and how we might satisfy them. The other side of Ruby's comment about the architect's deadline was the issue of finance. What was it going to cost to bring M into this world? I'd naively hoped that the first year wouldn't be too expensive. I'd roughly listed the costs for the first twelve months as being hospital fees, a cot, pram, and nappies. M would consume mostly breast milk and would wear mainly hand-me-downs and presents. So aside from the loss of Ruby's income while on maternity leave, I didn't anticipate any great cost output. I had a lot to learn.

We'd already lost money by cancelling an overseas holiday at late notice and now it looked like renovations were on the cards. Sure, we'd planned to do them eventually, but now they had to be done to accommodate a newborn. The being-a-parent list did not include a cancelled holiday and house renovations, and we hadn't even begun the first twelve months. All we'd done so far was see Ruby's GP. All the other stuff wasn't on Medicare.

These thoughts raised a multitude of other issues:

where the birth should take place;
who the obstetrician and midwife should be;
how to manage work, day care etc. when the child comes home;
where she (he) might go to school;
whether we should save for university fees now;
what's happening to M now;
what Ruby wants right now.

Only the last of the issues concerned me at the moment – cheese and tomato on toast.

FRUSTRATING BODILY CHANGES

In the days leading up to Christmas, life was a blur of end-of-year stress, constant nausea, no kisses (metallic breath), fights with the insurance company over cancellation of the Great Overseas Trip, Twisties, tiredness, shopping crowds and abstinence from alcohol. Ruby's taste buds were merrily doing their own thing. Tea and coffee made her nauseous. She couldn't believe she'd ever liked wine, sweet things repelled her, she couldn't be in the same room as fish, nectarines or shortbread, and the mere mention of chocolate brought her out in a cold sweat. She staggered around the house feeling tired and grumpy and with a constant pain in the pit of her stomach. She fought an onslaught of pimples on her chin and complained incessantly about her breasts.

This last issue was particularly frustrating, and not just for her.

'My breasts are killing me,' she'd say, 'they're getting so big.' Then she'd tuck a hand under each one to give them support. No red-blooded man I know can resist the sight of the woman he loves walking naked around the house cupping a breast in each hand. (In fact no red-blooded man I know can resist the sight of any woman walking naked around the house cupping a breast in each hand, but not any woman does that sort of thing these days. Unfortunately). To a man, we will, with good reason, interpret this as an invitation to sex.

'Look at them,' she'd say, thrusting eyefuls of breast at me. They were hypnotic. 'Come to me,' they seemed to say, their darkened areolae protruding like beacons on the edge of a succulent coastline. 'Make love to me,' I heard them say. My knees grew weak. Blood drained south from my brain. My breathing grew heavy, and my underpants were suddenly too small. At this stage a man's intent is all too obvious.

'Don't even think about it,' she'd say. 'They're too sore. My nipples itch. Can you believe it? I've got itchy nipples!' Little voices in my head said, 'Let me massage them'. Or at least I thought they were just in my head, because Ruby would typically observe, 'What is it with men and breasts? They're all the same. We all have them. You've seen one pair . . .' and she trailed off. For my part, if you've seen one pair you've *got* to see them all.

THE SEX THING

But Ruby was having none of it. She felt disgusting, her breasts hurt, my kisses tasted metallic, I stank even after I had a shower and she was increasingly tired. On most occasions the best sex we could muster looked a bit like it must when friends greet each other at a nudist camp: a quick peck on the cheek ensuring that no other body part makes contact. She felt the same frustration, on top of everything else, because in the odd moments things let up she would seize the opportunity for sex, usually after a plate of cheese and tomato on toast or a packet of Twisties.

'We can do it now,' she'd say and we'd down whatever tools we had at the time and maximise the opportunity. A case of *carpe diem*. But on most days it was, 'I'd love to, and I miss it, but I feel too disgusting.'

A HAPPY NEW YEAR

On Christmas Day I watched her push a piece of ham around the lunch plate and stare glumly at the glass of champagne as the bubbles faded. When friends came around in the evening she sat silently at the table, hands across her tummy until she finally excused herself early for bed. The year sauntered towards a very average end. Ruby began to sleep properly but cystitis and thrush had joined the litany of ills which plagued her. Because we weren't able to go overseas we decided to have a holiday in Australia. This would give us a break while still having competent medical support within reach. We decided to have two weeks in Victoria followed by two in Tasmania. We'd do some walking if Ruby was up to it or just rest and feel sick if not.

As the plane lifted at takeoff, Ruby groaned and closed her eyes. She murmured that the whole plane was spinning, and I reached for the sick bag among the in-flight magazines, headphones and safety cards in the seat pocket. She set up camp in bed in our Melbourne hotel, complaining of a cold. We dressed her in thermals and my polar fleece and covered her in four blankets, but she still felt chilled and feverish.

'I'm scared,' she stammered, and the tears flowed. 'I don't want anything to happen to the baby.' Part of this was the fear she may have done something to damage the embryo. 'I didn't know I was pregnant in the first month,' she said. 'I could've done anything. What about the herbs the naturopath gave me? I don't know if they're safe. Or the trek training we were doing. Or the parties we went to. ' I was confident of Ruby's generally robust state of health and told myself this was just morning sickness, possibly combined with the release of all that Christmas stress. I didn't think there was any serious complication. But what would I know?

I chased down one of the few doctors left in the city over the New Year weekend, and managed to drag Ruby out to see him. He assured us that her illness was just morning sickness and a urinary tract infection, nothing more. He took a urine sample, prescribed amoxyl (an antibiotic he assured us was safe for pregnant women) and advised rest and sleep. We returned to the hotel and Ruby burrowed beneath the blankets and fell asleep.

I filled in time walking through the Botanic Gardens and nearby streets. A chilly breeze sprang up in the late evening. The anticipation of New Year's Eve festivities hung in the air. People strolled along the streets carrying bottles of wine. Groups were gathering as parties began. Cars headed towards the city packed with people planning to claim a good view of the fireworks. The cool breeze stepped up as the day darkened. I felt this city had nothing to offer me, with everything closed, none of my friends around, the weather turning cold and my wife sick in bed.

She was awake when I returned and ate a slice of the pizza I'd bought on the way home – a Margherita – good old tomato and mozzarella cheese. She looked a little better, and mustered the strength to climb to the rooftop patio of our hotel to welcome in the new year. Another couple was there with a bottle of champagne. 'Happy New Year!' they shouted merrily. We watched bits of the distant fireworks through the city buildings. I held Ruby in my arms, and whispered, 'Happy New Year.' She looked up at me, her face white in the darkness and said, 'I don't like being pregnant.'

'We'll leave tomorrow,' I replied. 'We'll head out on the Great Ocean Road and relax a bit. Hopefully that'll make things better.'

That was approximately the end of Month Two. Not a happy conclusion. Sick and tired, even angry at the experience, we wandered down to bed. It had not weakened our resolve. We'd started the process and were compelled to – wanted to – finish it, but we were burdened by the adverse effects it seemed to have upon us, especially upon Ruby. We'd heard it was usual for things to ease at the end of the third month. We had a month's holiday to wait it out.

What's happening to it

Month Two About 4 cm. Golf ball.

VITAL STATISTICS

Length: About 4 centimetres. The length is measured according to the CRL (cranial/rump length), i.e. head to bum.

Weight: About 15 grams.

Brain: Still developing. About half the length of the foetus. At this stage it's smooth, not wrinkled like ours.

Heart: Still beating. All the other organs are in place.

Backbone: More like a plastic rod, with vertebrae beginning to grow on a basic spinal cord. Ribs have begun to appear.

Skin: Two layers of skin have begun to develop, but both are almost transparent.

Eyes: Skin covering the cup of the eyestalk becomes the retina. Inside the cup a lens and cornea are forming. The surrounding skin becomes the eyelid.

Ears / Hearing: The primitive shape of the outer ear appears on the skin. There's further development of the middle and inner ear.

Limbs: Buds appear early in the month, like little webbed ping pong paddles for hands. The feet appear a few days later, in a very similar shape.

Sex: There's a tiny protrusion between the legs that, under a microscope, looks like a penis with a vagina along its underside. There are two slight swellings on either side which are future ovaries or *testes*.

What's happening to her

Morning sickness will probably be in full swing. Not all women get it, although most get some form. It can be anything from feeling woozy to incessant vomiting. Ask your obstetrician about what can be done and what can be ingested, especially if it's severe. The most helpful things seem to be:

- Eating small meals frequently. There's a fine line between staving off the nausea and giving it too much fuel to throw back up, but keeping a small amount of food in the stomach seems to help, like dry biscuits and toast.

- Rest, sleep, lie down.

- TLC from the father, including, unfortunately, lots of help with day-to-day chores: cooking, cleaning, everything. With her in bed, the house is ours to keep, but up to her standards. Yawn.

- Time to focus just on the pregnancy. Freedom from having to worry about the washing up, work and other things in her life: e.g. see previous point. Double yawn.

- Enough pleasurable activities to divert her attention. Things like picnics, movies etc. Sex, possibly. Some pregnant women want it, others can't stand the idea.

- Drinking water to rehydrate, especially if vomiting.

Food cravings may also be happening. These can get weird. Some women want sweet, some want savoury. Sometimes she'll eat like a horse despite the nausea, scoffing down a breakfast of four slices of toast, four eggs, half a pig of bacon, grilled tomatoes, mushrooms and spinach, whatever. The little one might only be 3 to 4 centimetres long, but it demands a lot. Often she'll eat a mound of the same stuff like five slices of cheese on toast. Whatever she eats, just go with the flow, particularly when it flows back up again.

Her senses may change, particularly taste and smell. The flip side of food cravings is a prohibition on certain tastes. If she likes sweet she'll hate savoury and vice versa. Some women will drop tea and coffee altogether, while others find particular foods like cauliflower, chocolate or apples totally revolting. The same goes for smell. Some things will be totally and suddenly abhorrent. One friend's wife told him to buy a new car because the old one stank.

Medical/vaginal upsets.
She may suffer a range of things that can cause discomfort to her vaginal area, such as thrush and cystitis. These should be checked by her regular doctor if not the obstetrician.

Fatigue.
If she wasn't tired during Month One, she most likely will be during Months Two and Three. This human building is tiring work.

Urination.
She may find herself going to the loo many more times than before.

Flatulence.
Combined with excessive vomiting and weeing, she can get the farts really easily. Just remind yourself, and her, how beautiful she looks, not smells.

Breasts.
Hey, yeah, the breasts are getting bigger.

Depression.
This may develop due to both physiological and emotional changes. Hormones surging through her body will have an impact on her as they build the baby. Also, she's going through a huge emotional journey: all the thoughts and fears of parenthood, but exacerbated even more by the hormonal changes. All the books advise making use of the time available to talk, support and rest, and to start creating the spirit of family.

Irritability.
She's also likely at times to be very moody. The first trimester can be like three months of PMT. It can take extra care, patience and vigilance to survive and to support. Duck and weave a path to peace wherever possible. Discretion is the better part of valour. Have faith, it will end.

Other things she might be going through include a build-up of saliva, a runny nose, the shakes, constipation and a whole host of related nasties. It's weird watching it all go on. Be prepared for anything and be on the lookout for anything which might look serious.

A FINAL WORD ON MORNING SICKNESS

It's odd but none of the books seemed to be able to really explain what causes morning sickness. Most just say it happens, which is comforting to most mothers I'm sure. One of the most interesting theories I came across is in a book by Robert Winston called *Human Instinct* (Bantam Press, 2002). He's the guy who made his name doing the *Human Body* video I mentioned in Month One, and this book comes from another series he did on the extent to which our evolutionary past influences our current behaviour. In short, his theory goes a little like this:

> To counteract illness and death from parasites and other bugs in food, our apeman ancestors all those millions of years ago developed different layers of biological defence mechanisms which may be roughly categorised under three headings:
>
> 1) Our senses: a bad piece of meat looks the wrong colour, smells off, is slimy and if we are foolish enough to taste it, tastes foul;
>
> 2) Vomiting, diarrhoea etc.: if we eat it, we'll throw up, or get the runs;
>
> 3) Our immune system: any bugs that enter our system will be counter-attacked by the body's natural internal defence mechanisms.

The problem is that particularly in the first trimester, the mother's immune system is lowered so it won't reject the incoming foetus. As a result she has to rely more on the first two defences. She's more highly attuned to things smelling rank or tasting foul, to minimise the risk that anything bad might enter her body and injure her little one. Thus, to her senses, fine wine smells like pig-swill and a good snog tastes revolting. And when she does eat, because she has to, she'll get rid of it as quickly as possible in case it's suspect. She's basically doing what has been deeply inscribed in her genes by our ancestors on the African savannah.

At the end of the third month the little baby is pretty well established, and the mother's internal mechanisms ease up a bit, now prepared to take the risk that the more robust little foetus is able to cope with the regular smorgasbord we eat from day to day. As to why some women have a harder time of it than others, the explanation can only be that in all these genetically inscribed things, there is a variation from individual to individual, in the same way that we can all run, but some people can do it better than others.

So you can tell her all this as she retches into the toilet bowl. No doubt she (and you) will find it helpful to blame it all on some half-ape half-man eons ago, and not the one standing next to her who got her into this condition in the first place.

What's happening to me

OUR FIRST FAMILY HOLIDAY

A miserable rain-sodden morning transformed into a brilliantly sunny day as we drove out of Melbourne along the winding vistas of the Great Ocean Road. As we cruised along the cliff-encrusted coastline, I wondered how Ruby would take the drive. My mother had often regaled me with the story of how, when I was a mere skerrick of a boy, she and I had walked virtually the whole road to Apollo Bay because I vomited every time I got into the car. Now, some 35 years later, I was concerned at the effect of the drive upon my own tiny child-to-be, and its mother. After cramps, nausea, thrush and general illness in Melbourne, I wondered if the windy road might tip her over the edge, so to speak. Liftoff in the plane from Sydney had sent her brain spinning like a gyroscope, the roads might do the same, and the rental car garbage bag was nowhere in sight. I glanced at her impassive face shielded by dark sunglasses in the passenger seat next to me and asked how she was.

There was no reply. I looked her way again. She wasn't moving.

'Are you feeling okay?' I asked. Silence and the burr of the road beneath us. I wondered how far I should push the issue.

'Not sick?' I asked. The blue seas of Bass Strait entered and left my field of vision. Ruby seemed not to notice. One more try, I thought, just in case I have to find somewhere to pull over quickly.

'You still with us?' Her head turned heavily towards me.

'The drive is making me very sleepy,' she mumbled drowsily. 'I can hardly keep my head upright.' I reached over and took her hand in mine. It was limp with sleep. The rocking of the car was affecting her which was not a bad thing when all was said and done. A snooze might do her good.

I drove on, content in my own thoughts, getting to know how the cruise control worked in the hire car. By a stroke of good luck we'd been gratuitously upgraded to a family-sized Falcon with all the add-ons: airbags, climate- and cruise-control and thumb controls on the steering wheel.

I'd figured out I could control the car without using the foot pedal by clicking the off and re-set buttons on the cruise control. By clicking it off at a sufficient distance before a corner, the car would gradually slow enough for me to take the corner without applying the brake. When we were almost around the bend I would click re-set and the car would surge to its re-set speed. I set myself the challenge to travel the whole of the Great Ocean Road to Apollo Bay, clicking only the cruise control buttons, except maybe when we came to townships with traffic lights. I told myself this would provide a smoother ride for Ruby than braking all the time. So I clicked off and felt the car slow before a turn. Then I clicked on and felt the sudden thrust of the engine pull me forward again. Click off. Click on. This was cool. Click off. Click on. Ruby's head swivelled towards me.

'What're you doing?' she asked.

'What do you mean?'

'All that clicking. It's driving me nuts.'

'I'm using cruise control,' I explained. 'You've got to practise these things.'

'Well don't,' she said. 'Cruise control is for flat straight bits like freeways, so you don't get caught speeding.' She jammed her jumper between her head and the window and turned her back to me. So much for that idea, and we hadn't even reached Lorne. Perhaps I should just enjoy the scenery.

To our right, cliffs and steep hills alternated with rolling farmland. To the left the coast disappeared and reappeared, a mixture of cream beaches and windblown scrub. At every major inlet or town I could see family groups playing on the water's edge or swimming in the shallows. Coloured beach umbrellas dotted the flat sands and city-white fathers stood ankle deep in the water with toddlers splashing between their legs. We were travelling to Family Holiday World. The safe and pretty beaches were an easy drive (or walk for the car-sick toddler) from the city, and provided both endless recreation for boisterous children and stress relief for their parents. I hadn't been in Family Holiday World for ages. Not since I was a little boy when I whiled away the hours squealing at purple crabs in rocky pools or burying Daddy's legs in the sand. For the last twenty or so years my vacations had been adventure holidays, like Nepalese trekking and orang-utan spotting in Kalimantan. I would return from my various trips revitalised and fit, breathing sea-level air with high-altitude lungs and viewing city highlights with a mountain mind.

But the crystal coastline of southern Victoria was not Nepal. This was not going to be an adventure holiday. Driving along as Ruby slumbered beside me, I knew I would spend a great deal of this holiday waiting. Waiting for when she might feel well enough to be able to do something, waiting for her to finish resting, waiting as the baby brewed. It would be a time for attending to Ruby's needs. Making breakfast, cups of tea in the vain hope that she might want one after all, taking a slow stroll, carrying all the loads, reading while she slept, and just chatting while she was awake. If M allowed us to go bush walking or explore the Twelve Apostles, we would. If she(he) didn't, we'd stay in our room or on our verandah and let time tell us how long a day is, or a week, or a month of a tiny growing child. This would be a family holiday, but without a family yet.

RUMINATING A BIT

Driving along without cruise control and with a sleepy companion, I had only my thoughts and the occasional slow car in front to occupy me. I suddenly felt very old. This was obviously another one of those new things that pregnancy was bringing out in me. I was very conscious of getting older. This was a new thought. In your late thirties, you can't party all night, you can't kick a ball as high or run as fast, and you aren't as flexible as you once were, or as thin. Even the photo on your drivers licence isn't you. And there are junior members of staff who are, God forbid, half your age. People born after the Vietnam War, who never knew life without CDs or PCs. So long as you don't try playing any competitive sport against them, you can ignore this and tell yourself that, mentally at least, you're just as fit as the rest of them, and can drink with the best, even if you're old enough to know when it's time to stop. Basically, you feel as young as you are at the moment. Tomorrow is going to be as good as today, if not better. You live in the now and after, not in the past.

But now, as I reflected on whether or not to overtake the farting rust heap crawling in front of me, there would always be a little part of me that was younger than I was: my child. No matter how young I might feel, I would always be older than M (about 40 years older in fact). And however much I might try to fudge the age differences between myself and younger kids at work, I would never be able to fudge the age gap with M. M was a definite reminder that time was passing. I don't know, perhaps we measure time by significant moments of change in our lives, like going to school, leaving school, the first job, the first mortgage, getting married. On all these fronts it had been a fair time since I'd passed through a significant change. And a first child was certainly a big one. Or perhaps this was just my DNA talking, reminding me that I had now replicated myself, that biologically I was history, as my genes were now about to be carried forward by someone else. Or perhaps feeling old was just part of being a parent. Oo–er.

When friends of mine found out they were going to be fathers, they'd exclaimed, 'Imagine me, old enough to be a father!' They weren't doubting their physical ability to actually produce a kid, but acknowledging the same feeling of age. Associated with it is a feeling of responsibility. Suddenly your carefree days are over. You have a family to care for. You can't just get up and leave a job, or the city you live in to go travelling, or for a change of career: you have dependants to consider. What you do affects how they live, and what futures they might have. It's all a bit daunting really. You have to behave like parents.

Which was also a bit daunting, because the only real role model you have for being a parent is your own pair of oldies. What if you don't like the way they did it? What was right and wrong, good or bad, compassionate or harsh about your upbringing? What would you do better, and how will you know how to do it? And don't forget, the rules will be different for your children, so you'll have to adapt to the times. They'll face new pressures, play with new technologies, and be totally different people from you. What you want might not be right for them.

Not that I didn't feel ready to have children. I was ready. I wanted them. Well, a child anyway. Well, sort of ready. I could feel ready, because I knew bugger-all about the process of having a child, feeding it, raising it, educating it, showing it life's little trickeries and investing it with delight and confidence. In fact the more I thought about it the less I felt ready, and only seven months to prepare. Oh dear – was I ready or not? What I was ready for was to move on from the childless life, but what I needed much more preparation for was taking on the childed life. Which, like a child playing hide and seek, was coming, ready or not.

PLAYING CARETAKER

I had no memory of Apollo Bay from my childhood, so the peaceful open safety of the beach was a novelty. There was no surf to speak of and we could see the small cluster of beachgoers braving the cool afternoon breeze on the sands or in the water. We checked into what turned out to be a grossly overpriced and under-serviced motel at the western end of the Bay, put on our swimming costumes and ambled across to the beach. The water was freezing. We lasted five minutes, before heading back around the golf course to the motel. On the way Ruby stopped, bent over.

'My nipples are freezing!' she complained. 'They're so cold they're burning.' She put on her denim jacket and raced back to our room for a hot shower and a cup of hot water with a slice of lemon.

The next day we felt well enough for a day's walk around Cape Otway. It was relatively flat with only a descent to the beach, but even here M was controlling operations. Normally an enthusiastic and strong walker, Ruby walked at a slow even pace behind me, focussing on quelling the nausea and not tiring herself too quickly. The walk lasted three hours, including a stroll along the beach, but Ruby was exhausted by the end of it. She was in bed by 8.00 pm that night. I read.

We got up late. Ruby had dry toast and half a bowl of rice bubbles. And a cup of hot water and lemon. Even though it was the height of summer, the Twelve Apostles were surrounded by grey clouds and buffeted by cold winds. Ruby rugged up and strolled from lookout to lookout, wearing an expression of patience almost as enduring as the yellow cliffs. As we gazed upon the majestic sea-washed statues, Ruby yelled through the wind, 'I need some dry bickies!' We returned to the car and she rummaged among the bags in the backseat. 'I'm learning how to do this. If I start feeling nauseous, I eat a dry biscuit and it goes away. Come on, let's go down to the beach.'

After a few days on the coast we headed north to a farmhouse on the western side of the Grampians. The first morning there, we got up at 8.00 am, anticipating a day's walk in the mountains. Ruby consumed an egg and toast, then turned to me and said, 'I think I'm ready for bed now,' and padded back into the bedroom. So I read, and patted the friendly border collie who sat by the door for most of the day. Then I washed the dishes. I examined the map of the Grampians. I did a load of washing. I patted the dog again. I inspected the chooks. I looked at the grey caps of the Grampians looming above me to the east. I patted the dog. I read about the walks we could do. I patted the dog. Occasionally she was awake long enough for a short bush walk or a stroll.

To cut a long story short, this was the prevailing pattern of this part of the holiday. Sleep. Breakfast. Sleep. Pat dog. Drive. Sleep. Walk. Drive. Sleep. Eat. Watch TV. Pat dog. Sleep.

'I can't believe how much I'm sleeping,' she said.

'You're brewing a baby,' I said. 'It's baby-brewing sleep. You're brewing M.'

'Come to bed with me,' she said. 'I want to cuddle you while I fall asleep.'

THE SEX THING AGAIN, AND BODILY FUNCTIONS

We lay down. She wrapped her arms around me and nestled her head on my shoulder. Sometimes it seemed as if we might have sex, but on most of these occasions (although not all) she was too tired, or the thrush had reappeared adding discomfort to fatigue. So I lay on the bed reading, while she slept next to me, her warm breath tickling the nape of my neck.

On one occasion she said to me, 'What I'd really like' – and I thought, a massage maybe, or a pain free labour – 'is to do a really big poo. I haven't been to the toilet for days.' Constipation, it seemed, had joined the catalogue of pregnancy woes. This was no doubt exacerbated by the return of her appetite. The craving for cheese and tomato flavoured meals had expanded to a craving for just about every form of food available in the region. So it was bacon and eggs in the morning, salad rolls for the walks, vanilla slices, ice-creams and soft drinks after a walk, a full meal each evening with chocolate during the video at night. The only things she couldn't stomach were tea, coffee and alcohol.

This caused some perplexity at the wineries we visited in the Pyrenees Region. Typically, the wine demonstrator would pour two tasting samples and on every occasion Ruby would dip her nose into the glass, and say, 'I'll just smell it. I can't drink it. It tastes foul.' We never worked out whether the wine men were insulted or confused, but at least we knew Ruby's sense of smell had returned.

The yellow hillsides and quaint old cottages of Daylesford provided more opportunity for Ruby's brewing sleep. She emerged from the bathroom of our cottage, fists held high, and declared with relief, 'Victory! We have a motion! The first in four days!' We celebrated by flying to Tasmania that morning.

The second half of our baby brewing holiday, Tasmania, was colder than the Victorian coastline. Even though it was summer, a biting chill accompanied most mornings and occasional rain dampened our outdoor plans. By chance we caught the Nineteenth Annual Cygnet Folk Festival, full of ferals, banjos and bodrums, before heading up to a friend's farmhouse in Ouse.

The Bells were a family of four daughters, the oldest of whom was about to turn 21. 'I'm thinking of buying a marquee,' Martin, the only man in the household, said to me as the younger two daughters teased and tied his grey hair into odd shapes. 'I figure I've got three functions for each of them: a twenty-first, probably an engagement party and a wedding.'

In 21 years time I'll be 60 I thought, and was reminded of my contemplations of age. Better get a marquee.

SICK OF FISHING

We went trout fishing the next day in a hydro pond 50 kilometres into the high country. It was a shallow man-made lake, desolate with the grey stumps of cut and drowned trees that stood in the clear waters like ruined columns of an ancient temple. Sunk in our waders, Martin and I set about hunting the flitting trout in the shallow water. Ruby fell asleep on the bank. We hid behind the stumps and moved slowly about the pond, occasionally casting our flies and trying to corral a fish on to a line. After about an hour, I heard Ruby coo-eee across the water. We were some distance away, so it took a good while to wade to the bank where Ruby was lying in a foetal position on the ground, clutching her stomach, eyes tight shut. She was on the verge of tears.

The craving for cheese and tomato flavoured meals had expanded to a craving for just about every form of food available in the region. So it was bacon and eggs in the morning, salad rolls for the walks, vanilla slices, ice-creams and soft drinks after a walk, a full meal each evening with chocolate during the video at night. The only things she couldn't stomach were tea, coffee and alcohol.

'I've got the most terrible cramps,' she groaned. 'I didn't want to interrupt you guys but I just can't stand it. They've never been this bad. I'm scared again.'

I held her and offered what little comfort I could. She was able to muster a slow bent shuffle for the kilometre walk to the car. Back at the farmhouse we tucked her into bed where she slept some more. That evening Martin's daughters waited on her with bowls of soup and bread, fully demonstrating the benefits of available and friendly care. We wouldn't have had this in Nepal. Ruby was feeling better although still a little sore when I joined her later in the evening. But she was feeling the emotional strain as this was shaping up to be a repeat of Melbourne. The third month was hard going, it seemed, and she was worried that it might not let up at all during the pregnancy. We lay in bed touching lightly, as a full hug was too unsettling for her.

'I had this silly hope that I'd have a dream pregnancy,' she said to me. 'That I would glow and be radiant and feel wonderful. It was only a hope, but this is awful.'

As she fell asleep I lay wondering what more I could do to help her. I couldn't hold her or hug her too much because it hurt her. I couldn't take her out because she was too tired. I couldn't cook her meals because she was too sick. Her appetite had been damaged by the cramps. The best I could do was be with her as the baby brewed, wait as she slept, woke and wandered through the days. I recalled Guru Dave saying to me that the father is an assistant during pregnancy, a coach at the birth and an assistant again for at least six months afterwards.

The next morning she said she felt stronger, so we decided to head for the highlands of Lake St Clair and maybe even Strahan. But at Lake St Clair the cramps kicked in again along with a sudden and savage twinge of cystitis. We hadn't gone twenty steps towards the lake before Ruby sat down on a bench and burst into tears. She hid from the crowd behind her sunglasses, her hat tugged down low, her collar pulled up and her head bowed into my shoulders. Her back jerked with the sobs of frustration. For someone who trekked up mountains for holidays, who ran six kilometres a day and led a generally pain-free, active and healthy life this was too much. I said, 'I don't think you're strong enough to make it to Strahan. Do you want to go home?'

She nodded. 'I'm worried we're wasting our time trying to have a holiday.'

'We can fly back home now and take an extra week's holiday later in the year when you feel stronger,' I suggested. 'You can be just as sick at home.' I held her close in my arms as we slowly walked back to the car. I figured we'd arrive too late at Hobart to catch a plane to Sydney that day, so I took her to Richmond, which is an old convict town just outside the airport. Perhaps if she felt stronger in the morning, we could decide to stay and if not, we could go first thing to the airport. I drove as smoothly as I could along the mountain road and the winding route lulled her into an uneasy sleep.

CLIMBING OUT OF THE FIRST TRIMESTER

Happily, next morning Ruby had revived and was her Grampian self. Keen to explore, keen to complete our holiday, albeit at a leisurely pace. Cheese and tomato on toast was back on the menu with a cup of hot water with lemon. The week was spent at Port Arthur. Next, north to the vast blue bays of Freycinet Peninsula and finally, down to Mount Field National Park. A fair bit of driving allowed Ruby some good sleeping time between days of walking and sight-seeing. She'd learned how to regulate her tiredness, so we stopped when she needed to, ate what she could stomach and went to bed early.

By the time we reached Mount Field National Park, Ruby was strong enough to complete our holiday with a five-hour walk in the alpine regions of the Park. This involved an exhilarating climb around the icy tarns and blanched trees of the mountain before descending again. Even though Ruby took it slowly, it was clear she was recovering her strength. The following day when we flew out, the plane didn't turn her stomach. Approaching the end of the first trimester Ruby's health had improved. She wasn't totally recovered but her spirits had lifted and with it the anticipation of the coming months. The third month concluded with a reward for all the discomfort Ruby had suffered in the previous two months: our first ultrasound.

SEEING M: THE FIRST ULTRASOUND

Ruby had booked the ultrasound at Prince of Wales Hospital. Given that all hospitals have a sterile functionality about them, this wasn't too bad. Some parts of the floor even had carpet. We sat with four or five other pregnant couples waiting our call. A little boy ignored the (surprisingly un-battered) toys in the corner and tried to extract all the water from the cooler by the cupful, before his grandmother removed him kicking and screaming to the corridor. Kids, eh. Who'd have 'em.

The other stupid thing was the magazines on the coffee table: *Country Life,* (devoted to snooty rural life in Britain), *The High Life,* (devoted to snooty rural life in Sydney's Southern Highlands) and *Majesty,* (devoted to snooty royal life in Britain). God knows why. Does your brain turn to mush when you get pregnant?

The receptionist was a friendly woman with a reassuring air about her. Her job was predominantly dealing with nervous, happy people. She offered us the option of a video of the ultrasound. Only $11 extra. A video? A moving record of little M at three months. Was I going to succumb? Was I actually going to start the photographic record this early? And for only $11?

Of course I was. We bought the video.

Little waterboy was back at the cooler again distributing cups of refreshing spring water to all and sundry when someone called our name. This was it!

We passed through one of those mysteriously bland doors that hospitals always have, down an equally mysterious and bland corridor, through another door into a small darkened room. There was a reclining couch, a spare chair, a small stack of electronic equipment and a TV – a kind of home entertainment complex. There was also a second TV suspended from the ceiling above the door so Ruby could watch what was going on.

The ultrasoundographer (really called a sonographer) was typical of many hospital staff. She was warm, welcoming, but also focussed on the need to maintain patient turnover without making us feel too hurried as well as not missing any issues that might arise. Ruby lay on her back on the couch, her white tummy exposed for a blob of greenish gel. The sonographer fiddled with the machine, slotted our video into the tape recorder and massaged the gel across Ruby's belly with the hand-sized ultrasound unit.

The screen above us blinked into a fuzz of snowflake patterns like a badly-tuned TV. The sonographer moved the unit around and suddenly a tiny silver shape appeared: head, arms, legs, and little baby's bum sticking up in the air. Well, sticking up in the uterus anyway.

'There's your little one,' said the sonographer, and we were silent, captivated by the sight of our M. Strangely, my heart didn't leap as I'd expected, but I was enthralled by the little black and white image surrounded by the dark walls of what must be Ruby's uterus. What struck me most was the individuality of it. This was a creature, an infant human in its own little right . . . not me, not Ruby, not even part of us but made from us.

The sonographer asked, 'Is this your first?' One of us said yes. Wasn't it obvious? 'Let's wake it up,' she said and began kneading Ruby's belly to turn M into the right position. I watched transfixed as the baby somersaulted and rolled about the spongy dark walls of its uterine world. We saw the brain hemispheres, the beating heart, the spine and incipient ribs glowing on the screen like dewy spider webs. M's arms floated effortlessly in an outstretched fashion, his(her) little ankles crossed behind his(her) pointed bottom. The umbilical cord lit up momentarily as the only coloured item on the screen. From head to rump the baby measured 6.2 centimetres and its heart pattered at 168 beats per minute. In one position M seemed to be leaning against the wall of the uterus looking out, much like an old lady might do from an upstairs window, looking back at us from inside the video screen. That is, if it was a she. I was too fascinated by everything that was going on to look more closely for evidence of gender. Besides, when is gender determined? Would we be able to find out at twelve weeks?

The placenta was healthy, the cervix closed. The baby was developing normally. Ruby was doing a great job. Months of Twisties, hot water, thrush, nausea, cystitis, fatigue, cramps, folk music, aeroplane rides and winding roads had had no effect on resilient little M. Instead the baby spun around in its little control room like a spaceman on a space walk. Here at last was confirmation that something was really happening. Sure the urine test said it was true, but who's going to trust a drop of wee to tell them the future? And sure, the nausea, irritability, tiredness and cramps had said it was too, but who's going to tell the future from feeling disgusting? Here we were seeing it live on ultrasound, compensation for all Ruby had gone through so far. I was glad we bought the video.

The radiologist, Doctor Tubby, came to tell us what all the various measurements meant. Basically, everything was healthy. The one in 1,963 chance of Down's Syndrome was at the safe end of the spectrum although we felt dubious. Gambling addicts throw away their livelihoods on odds far worse than that. However, I reasoned this wouldn't be the first time we'd need to put our trust in medical expertise.

We strode out of the hospital glowing. M was on track doing what prenates are supposed to do, that is, grow. All the support systems were in place. As programmed, the first trimester had constructed spinal column, brain, heart and limbs as well as a healthy placenta. In the car park Ruby turned to me with her enormous grin, something that I'd been missing all month. It took a moment to realise what she said.

'Bugger. It's only one. I was hoping for twins. Get it all over and done with in one hit.'

'Dream on,' I said, 'twins are never easier. Let's get this one done before we start thinking about the next.'

What's happening to it

Month Three About 7–8 cm. Tennis ball.

VITAL STATISTICS

Length: About 7–8 centimetres.

Weight: About 30 grams.

Brain: Forms about half to one-third of the foetus.

Bones: Growing.

Eyes: Everything has been made. The eyelids close, stored for future use.

Ears / Hearing: Still developing. The outside ear is still formative.

Limbs: Everything is a little bigger. Fingers and toes begin to emerge from the ping pong paddles.

Hair: The first whiskers on the body of the embryo appear.

Sex: A vagina appears, or a penis, although they are too small to be seen on an ultrasound. Both ovaries and testes are inside the abdomen. Early ova and primitive sperm are forming.

Skin: Still developing.

What's happening to her

See Months One and Two for the litany of ills and upsets such as morning sickness, fatigue and food cravings. If all goes well it should calm down by the end of this month.

Don't forget the emotional weariness she may be feeling. How are you both going? Have you seen your obstetrician lately? Have you prepared a list of questions to ask him/her?

She (i.e.the mother) will probably have started to show by now with a small but visible bump on the front of her tummy. Some of her clothes will become too tight and it will be time to think about a pregnancy wardrobe.

There's likely to be some weight gain associated with the increasing Frontal Bump. Weight gain varies from mother to mother. There are no hard and fast rules here. A doctor or a nutritionist can advise best. As a rule of thumb, she'll put on anywhere between ten and fifteen kilograms over the pregnancy, depending on her starting size. About one third of that will be the baby, placenta and associated stuff in the womb. The rest will be hers to look splendid with afterwards. And no, she doesn't look fat in that.

MORE ABOUT THAT ULTRASOUND

It's common practice for an *ultrasound* to take place towards the end of the first trimester, around week twelve or thirteen (although it can be a bit later depending on your work commitments etc.). An ultrasound involves a harmless examination of the foetus using sound waves to construct a picture of the baby. It therefore avoids the impacts of X-rays on the growing foetus. The images on the TV screen look a bit like a black and white video shot during a blizzard. When you look at someone else's ultrasound stills you can never make out what is head and what is feet, but when it comes to your own child, it's somehow all very clear and obvious.

The purpose of the Twelve-Week Ultrasound is essentially to check on foetal growth, assess the risk of any abnormality and carry out a measurement called the *nuchal translucency* measurement to assess the risk of Down's syndrome. The size of a fold at the back of the baby's neck is measured – to within one millimetre accuracy. This is then factored into the age and health of the mother to give a risk assessment of Down's syndrome. The parents can then decide if they want to go on to the *amniocentisis* test (see Month Four) which determines if Down's is present. For Ruby it was a one in 1,963 chance, which I thought was high risk, but apparently is fairly low. This figure is, at a later date, further clarified by comparison with blood tests, which usually confirms the likelihood is even lower in a healthy mother.

At this time they'll also usually measure the heartbeat, cranial-rump length and heart rate, and have a general look at the foetal development. They'll also check the interior of the womb (the cervix, uterus, *amniotic fluid* volume and the placenta). They can usually spot twins too, if they're there. In most cases there's another ultrasound at about eighteen weeks, when the foetus is large enough for the ultrasound to examine all the organs, limbs and inner workings of the baby in greater detail.

Did I say that ultrasound is harmless? It certainly appears to be. However, true to form, no doctor will actually say so. All the brochures will only say things like 'In 25 years of research and clinical use no adverse side-effects of ultrasound have been demonstrated'. I don't know if there are still panels of experts around the world looking for adverse side-effects, but it seems that every new parent-to-be has it, if only out of an overwhelming desire to see their kid as soon as possible.

CVS – CHORIONIC VILLOUS SAMPLING

The obstetrician may recommend tests at about twelve weeks (around the end of month three) to check for genetic disorders, depending on the family medical history, previous pregnancies and the findings of the nuchal translucency tests. The main test procedure, called *CVS* or *chorionic villous sampling*, involves taking a very small sample of the placenta from inside the womb. The procedure carries a slightly higher risk of miscarriage than amniocentesis. It was not recommended in our case.

Settling in

What's happening to me

PUBLIC AWARENESS GROWS

Into the second trimester. Guru Dave had warned me that the Pregnant One had a different emotional phase for each of the three trimesters: (1) Tired, (2) Powerhouse and (3) Fed Up. Ruby had been tired the first trimester. Would she fit the powerhouse bill the next? The thought of it horrified me. She was normally a powerhouse anyway without being preggers. If the kid inside her added extra kick, look out boyo. I had a vision of being forced to jog miles in the wee hours of the morning, do four loads of washing and clean the house before breakfast, double my work hours, party late, do charity work, chair committees and manage on twenty minutes sleep a night, just to keep up with Ruby. I contemplated having a will prepared.

THE 'BIG' ISSUE

As if on cue, Ruby's belly had bulged slightly, registering M's presence at three months. A small round pouch was showing, not enough to really alter Ruby's appearance or require a new wardrobe, but enough for those in the know to say, 'Oh you're showing'. Or enough for those not in the know to ask themselves, 'Is she pregnant?'. Or enough for Ruby to say, 'I feel so fat.'

She stood side on, in front of the mirror, holding her shirt above her tummy. 'Look at me,' she said, moving her hand over her stomach. 'I'm getting fat.' Of course she wasn't. She was just starting to show. Just starting to publicise the fact that we were going to be parents. And that I was going to be the father, if I hung around close enough for people to identify me as being half responsible for the bulge. I kissed her on the cheek and placed my hand on her tummy.

'You're not getting fat,' I said, 'you're pregnant. You're allowed to get bigger. In fact, you have to.'

71

'I know,' she said, 'but now everyone will know we've had sex.'

'Of course we have,' I said, 'that's how you get pregnant.'

'But when you're just in the street, no one knows,' she said. 'You can't tell if someone is having sex or not when you're out in public, but with us you can. People can look and say, you've had sex.' I could see her point, but it wasn't entirely true. There are some blokes at work who are as transparent as glass. They come into work wearing the biggest smiles if they've had it the night before, or that morning. And besides, so what? People have sex all the time. According to the *Human Body* video, there are 100 million acts of sexual intercourse that keep the world going round every day. That's over 1,150 per second in case you're wondering. No wonder the world spins. So, just for the record, I will state that I had sex with my wife, even before I got her pregnant. I'm a lucky bloke.

PLAYING CRICKET WITH THE OBSTETRICIAN

The first order of the trimester was to meet the obstetrician. This is the man to head the team on The Day. This meant of course that The Day was getting closer. Things had to be planned. Medical oversight of procedures had to be initiated. We had seen the target – M – had video surveillance in fact, and now had to begin to get her (him?) out. Dr Q was the man to lead the team for the job.

He was a suave looking dude, with an air of quiet unrufflability about him. He had a few grey flecks amongst his youthful shock of brown hair, and he focussed a reassuring gaze upon both of us from behind his spectacles as we entered his room.

'Come in,' he said, 'come in.' His handshake was firm and cordial. The thought flashed through my mind that this hand had groped many an infant's bloodied head from many a uterine cavity and had sewn together all sorts of torn delicacies. It was a skilled hand, and I hope he'd washed it. 'Sit down.' He sat behind his desk and rearranged the papers in front of him as he spoke. His movements were fluid and confident, like he could coax a hollow crystal baby from the most tenacious womb. He turned his gaze upon Ruby.

'How are you feeling?' She'd been tired, sick, exhausted, cystitis-ridden, nauseous etc. He listened with just a hint of an encouraging smile. All this was normal. He asked if we'd had the ultrasound. We pulled out the envelope containing the ultrasound stills, and his quick fingers flicked it open. He studied the photos and Dr Tubby's report.

'All healthy. A high rubella count, a healthy placenta, the right length. Let's listen to it shall we?'

In a single movement he came round from behind his desk, placed Ruby on her back with her belly exposed, covered her tummy with the bluey-green gel we'd seen before and was exploring the white bulge with a hand-held amplifier. 'This is not an ultrasound,' he explained. 'It's just an amplifier to pick up the heart beat.' He moved it around a little, trying to pick up a regular beating amongst the background crackle. We waited, and stifled the fear that he might not find anything. He moved the amplifier some more.

'Sometimes they like to hide,' he said, and his wry smile tipped slightly for added reassurance. More crackle ensued as he massaged Ruby's belly. I thought of people I knew who hadn't heard their babies, and who'd then had to face worse . . .

Then the heartbeat sounded out, like oars rowing in dark water. One-hundred and sixty-nine even steady beats per minute. M was there, seen last week, now heard. It was slightly alien in fact. This was Ruby's body Dr Q was examining, but that was not Ruby's heartbeat. Something was living separately inside her, an alien inside its mother ship. Oo-er.

Dr Q put down the machine, wiped the gel from Ruby's belly and resumed his seat without even a hint of triumph. These things impress the parents enough without him having to embellish them.

Ruby and I (well mainly Ruby) had prepared a list of questions. She extracted a crumpled piece of paper from her bag. 'I hope you can answer these for us.'

This was clearly a game Dr Q had played on many other occasions. He eyed us like an experienced batsman might a new bowler, confident he could cope with whatever we threw at him. Ruby launched the first question.

'Will the sickness I had in the last few months affect the baby?'

He played this with a straight bat.

'No, it was normal morning sickness,' he said. Ruby looked at her piece of paper.

'How about the things like cystitis and thrush?' she asked.

He turned this nicely past slips for some early runs.

'No, they won't affect the baby. They are common complaints during pregnancy and have no bearing on the development of the foetus.' Ruby focussed her attack.

'How about the amoxyl I was given in Melbourne?' she asked.

Dr Q pushed this one defensively past the keeper towards the boundary.

'That's fine. None of those types of drugs have shown any effect on pregnancy.' Ruby resorted to a more long-standing approach.

'And I have asthma – is there any likelihood of the baby being deformed or having to suffer because of that?'

A clear cover drive. He was in his element now.

'Nope. Your baby will not be affected.' It was as simple as that. Ruby tried again.

'I take Ventolin and Pulmicort. Will they have any effect?'

Easy pickings, straight to the boundary again.

'Nothing has ever been shown, and plenty of women take these while pregnant.' Ruby retreated to her list to look for something new.

'What about diet?' she asked. 'I've been told that I shouldn't eat things like sushi because it's not cooked, but I've really been craving it, and I know I ate some in the first month before I knew I was pregnant.'

A jaunty sweep to leg-on sent this one rattling for four.

'If it's fresh, that's fine. I wouldn't have it if it's been lying around for a day, but that applies whether you're pregnant or not.' Nothing seemed to fluster him. You could see him comfortably settled in. Ruby dug deeper.

'Last year, before I knew I was pregnant, I went to a herbalist for stomach cramps and he prescribed this list of stuff which I took.' She handed over a piece of paper. 'I thought you could check to see if they were okay.'

He surveyed the list:

> eye of newt
> tincture of toad's breath
> St John's wort
> smell of an oily rag . . .

It was a no ball, and he let it pass to the keeper.

'These mean nothing to me,' he said. 'You'd have to ask the herbalist. I only deal in chemical names. But if they are just herbs, I shouldn't worry too much.' Ruby tried a new approach.

'I had an acupuncturist who told me that if he put needles in my calves during labour, I would have a pain-free birth.'

This was his moment of triumph, and he knocked it for an easy six. You could almost hear the crowd roar. He fixed Ruby with his steely gaze, his lips curled and he read her the rules in the plainest English possible:

'You will not be having a pain-free labour.'

It was all over. Ruby, defeated, emitted a nervous little laugh and shrank back into her chair, forced to accept the awful truth of it. She would not be having a pain-free labour. She would be having a painful labour. Poor bugger, I thought selfishly. Glad it's not me. He did soften the blow a bit by adding, 'I usually find that these people are reluctant to come to your assistance at 3.00 am, or at 11.00 pm on a Sunday'. Clearly we weren't the first to raise the hope of a pain-free labour, and probably wouldn't be the last, but we all had to get our head around it. Labour is a painful process. It had an awful and random certainty about it. Certainty, because there would be pain. Random, because we didn't know when. Although it appeared not to be during normal business hours.

I took up the line of questions, in what I hoped was a more consultative tone of voice. 'What about exercise?' I asked. 'Is there any limit to the amount of physical activity Ruby can do? She's been going to the gym and bush walking. Is there anything we should not be doing?'

Dr Q turned his gaze to me. 'Not really,' he said. 'The healthier the mother is, the better the pregnancy. You can keep up your normal regime of exercise.'

'But is there anything we shouldn't do or be careful of?' I asked.

'I wouldn't do a marathon on a hot day,' he replied dryly.

So in her powerhouse phase, I wondered, was Ruby going to start running marathons? I made a mental note: add a 30-kilometre jog to my daily routine.

This was his moment of triumph, and he knocked it for an easy six. You could almost hear the crowd roar. He fixed Ruby with his steely gaze, his lips curled and he read her the rules in the plainest English possible: 'You will not be having a pain-free labour.'

FOOT IN MOUTH DISEASE

Leaving Dr Q's rooms Ruby was despondent. 'He didn't like the idea of no pain, did he?' she said.

'No,' I concurred, and then said one of those ridiculously stupid things which, immediately after you've said it, you know you've dug your own grave, laid down in it and pulled the earth in on top of you.

'You know, if I had to choose between attending the ultrasound or the birth – if someone said you can only go to one or the other but not both – I think I'd choose the ultrasound. It's cleaner, and doesn't sound nearly so gruelling.'

I have no idea of the logic behind it, and no idea of what could possibly have possessed me to say it. But I have a very clear recollection of being pummelled with furious fists, being called all sorts of angry names, being the subject of endless angry telephone calls to friends, and being on the receiving end of a complete scrubbing for a week or so. No conversation, no contact, no communication, and of course sex was totally out of the question. Flowers couldn't heal it, cards and kisses were useless, as were breakfasts in bed, daily head and foot massages and freshly cooked dinners. Even Tiger got more attention than I did.

Finally after a week of grovelling apologies and pleas for clemency I shouted, 'What am I supposed to do? I've apologised, admitted I'm wrong, done penance, been dog-kennelled, what more can I do?'

There was a pause before she said, 'You can buy a new car.'

'A what?' I said, stunned.

'A new car,' she repeated. But we already had a car.

'But we already have a car,' I said.

'It's a junk heap,' she said.

We had an ageing but still very functional automatic hatch, with power windows and capacity to attach a CD player if we had one. What more could you want? 'It goes. There's no rust. It has power windows. It has a tape deck,' I remonstrated.

'It's not the type that is the problem,' she said.

'So what is?'

'We need a new car for M,' she explained.

'For M?'

'Yes.'

'M won't know a car from her or his left ear. What will M care about a new car?' I asked. It seemed to me a rational question.

'It's not the type that's the problem.' Was this déjà vu?

'So what is?' I asked. It was. Déjà vu, that is.

'We need it for M.' Definitely déjà vu.

'M will be in a baby capsule on the back seat,' I said, 'and I know there's a mountain of stuff like prams and nappies, but they can fit in the back. Like everyone else's does.'

'But there's Tiger,' said Ruby.

'Tiger?'

'She can't go in the back with all the prams and nappies and things,' Ruby explained.

'She sits on the back seat now,' I said. 'She can stay there.'

'I don't want Tiger sitting in the back seat slobbering all over M, and she can't fit in the back with all the prams and nappies,' objected Ruby. Suddenly it dawned upon me. Dog in the back, kid in behind, Ruby in front and, presumably me somewhere, but given my current status in the household, I couldn't be sure where.

'So you want a station wagon?' I asked.

'Yes,' she exclaimed, as if I'd been slow on the uptake. 'So Tiger can go in the back, M in the passenger seat and us in the front.'

'Us in the front?' I asked, seizing upon the possibility that I might have at last been forgiven. Is this what I had to do to redeem myself – buy a car?

'If you behave yourself,' she replied.

So, forgiven at last, I submitted myself to the thuggery of the used car market to trade in our current decrepit set of wheels for a station wagon. I was to be branded a family man, with a family wagon, with a family. A kid, a dog, a wife and a wagon, if not in that order. The things you have to do.

GRANDMA, GRANDPA AND THE NEW CAR

Two weeks later we picked it up and drove it down to my parents' house to show it off, along with Ruby's burgeoning tummy and the ultrasound photos. Mum and Dad were on the balcony of their villa.

'Ooh, look at Ruby,' shouted Mum and rushed to cradle Ruby's tummy in her hands.

'Hello, Dad,' I said. 'We've got a new motor.'

'You're looking like the radiant mother-to-be,' exclaimed my father holding open the fly-wire door for us.

'V6, 2.8-litre station wagon,' I said, to no-one in particular.

'And what's this?' Mum said, pointing at the envelope containing the ultrasound stills.

'Photos of M,' said Ruby.

'We brought them here in the back seat of the new car,' I added.

'Photos?' said father, trapped on the balcony behind the door.

'You've got to show me first,' said Mum snatching the envelope from Ruby's hand.

'It's got cruise control too,' I said to the wall.

'You're not to let Dad see these first,' reiterated Mum. 'I'll just get my cup of tea and you can sit down and show me.'

'ABS brakes and sunroof,' I said.

'Let me see,' said Dad now stranded as the door closed in his face.

'It's parked downstairs,' I said.

'Oh look,' said Mum, 'it's little M in the ultrasound.'

'Where?' said Dad's voice.

'Outside the garage,' I said.

'In here, Father, come and see,' said Mum, now in charge as Dad finally worked his way through the door, put on his glasses and peered over her shoulder. I hadn't a chance as my two parents bickered like children over the ultrasound stills.

'Let me see,' said Dad.

'Don't grab,' said Mum clutching them to her breast.

'I'm just trying to see,' he said.

'All in good time,' she replied.

'What does it mean Ruby?'

'Yes, show us.'

And they cooed and ogled over the black and grey shapes in the pictures, M's tiny skull, beating heart, frail arms and flailing legs, the iridescent spine and cerebral hemispheres, the placenta, the uterine wall, and the last shot of M who seemed to be leaning on an arm like a traveller in the window of a time capsule, wondering when she(he) would arrive and what would be there when she(he) finally did. We're coming sweetheart, I said under my breath. So am I, she seemed to be saying in reply. Or he.

Later that night Ruby and I sat up in bed reading. She had a book called *Baby Love* by Robin Barker (Pan Macmillan, 1997), a highly recommended instruction manual on how to look after newborns. I was reading a book called *Your New Station Wagon*, a creased old instruction manual on how to operate our new car. Ruby leaned over and kissed me on the shoulder.

'It's got a great father,' she said.

'It's got cruise control,' I replied.

NESTING

We were living in a state of almost total disarray by this time, as we were preparing to move to the Grandrubies' to make way for the renovations. Most of our belongings were in boxes: we sat on the two remaining kitchen chairs to watch the TV which stood on the floor. We ate off the remaining two or three plates, using the remaining two or three sets of cutlery to eat food cooked in one frying pan or the last microwave bowl. We had a folding picnic table, our beds, some clothes, blank walls to stare at and vacant floor boards. In short, nothing but the kitchen sink. Only Tiger remained unaffected, sleeping on either her normal bed or ours, chasing cobwebs and sniffing in corners.

I mentioned our domestic constraints to a colleague who stated, 'Oh, you're nesting. I remember I was holding the back door when our first was born.' I presumed he wasn't in the labour ward at the time.

My mother once told me that when she came home with my sister she had to help Dad push the fridge back into place because he hadn't finished painting the kitchen in time.

It didn't feel like we were nesting. We'd planned the renovations, and decided we may as well do them before M arrived. There was no feeling of urgency, or that we had to get everything perfect before Bub. That's how subtle this thing is. You don't feel it: somehow you just do it. I thought of numerous friends who'd renovated, painted, added a room, bought a new fridge, put on a deck, put up a carport, all in time for the arrival of their first born. Why? Not for the kid. The kid wouldn't know a carport from a canary. After all, humans had given birth in the wild thousands of years before carports were invented. Not that Ruby intended giving birth in the carport.

So why do we do it? For ourselves. To create the atmosphere that, for whatever reason, we feel will make raising a child just that little bit easier. So that at 3.00 am on the fourteenth consecutive sleepless night as we warm the bottle for the vomiting screaming poo-machine that bears our DNA we can doggedly comfort ourselves with the fact that at least we have a flat bit of colourbond on four sticks with a new station wagon under it. Our little carport. Makes it all worthwhile.

We were going the whole hog. Only the front room would remain, and the rest would be rubble, to be rebuilt into a magnificent nursery palace for M's arrival. No doubt half the house would be in pastels and primary colours. Teddy bears would litter the floors. Mobiles suspended from every ceiling. A change-table in every room, and an automatic baby-burper in the kitchen. The other half of the house would be a nappy laundry, except perhaps one small corner for Tiger's bed, behind the washing machine. Not what we had originally planned, but what the hell, we'd have a carport if we needed to sleep in the car.

On the day we moved Ruby stood on the front porch smiling and rubbing her slightly rounded tummy. 'It's exciting isn't it?' she said, as I lugged the last two suitcases past her down the stairs. They fitted easily in the capacious rear of the new station wagon.

'What is?'

'Having a baby,' she replied, 'and a new house. To live in with my new husband, the new father of my new baby.' She put her arms around me and gave me a big hug. And for the first time I felt her tummy as a protuberance, signifying something – someone – was there. M, as a little lump. I pulled up her shirt and felt the smooth white mound. There was no kick, but clearly M was there.

'It's got bigger over the last month,' I observed, 'you're pregnant.'

'Up the duff,' she said, 'and it's all your fault.'

Yep, mea culpa, and proud of it too.

What's happening to it

Month Four About 15 cm. Pliers.

VITAL STATISTICS

Length: About 15 cms

Weight: About 200 grams

Brain: Half the length of the foetus.

Bones: Are appearing and becoming stronger.

Eyes: Closed for future use.

Ears / Hearing: Is developing. Looking more like an ear now. The inner-ear is about adult size.

Hair: A thin layer of hair called *lanugo* covers the body. No one is quite sure why. It may be for warmth or protection, but it stays around until about Month Eight or Nine.

Limbs:	Fairly well developed. Arms and legs start extending.
Sex:	The penis or vagina is in place. The girl's ovaries contain the four to five million ova that she will have all her life, releasing one each month from puberty to menopause.

What's happening to her

- Morning sickness. With any luck this will decrease and even disappear. For some, it stops almost on day one of Month Four. For others, it just recedes. For others, it doesn't ever stop.

- Many of the other adverse effects also decrease: urination, fatigue, constipation etc.

- The breasts still get bigger.

- She'll still be eating like a horse.

- She may experience some breathlessness as the womb expands and she's not used to it.

- Her gums may start to bleed a little, especially when brushing her teeth.

- She may well start complaining about being too fat for her clothes, because her tummy will have expanded. She's not fat, she's pregnant, but she may not appreciate this. A new wardrobe is about to appear.

- Sometimes pregnancy brain will kick in – an occasional lack of focus or forgetfulness. Where she put things, or where she was going.

For some, the second trimester can be a power phase. She starts to glow, she gets energy, feels great, looks great, smiles and is often very horny. It can be a fantastic three months.

AMNIOCENTESIS

In some circumstances the obstetrician will recommend amniocentesis around Month Four, for a more thorough look at foetal development. As the name suggests, this involves extracting a sample of the amniotic fluid. A whole range of things can be learned from the chemical make-up of the fluid. Amneocentesis is particularly useful in assessing the risk associated with Down's syndrome, but also other things such as general chromosomal abnormalities, genetic disorders, some hereditary issues, and where the ultrasound suggests that further inquiry is warranted. It's usually not recommended if the mother is under 35 years of age, and if older, it's discussed beforehand.

The procedure involves passing a long needle through the mother's abdominal wall, and with the help of an ultrasound, extracting a sample of amniotic fluid. Having an 'amnio' is considered a bit risky, mainly because it involves intruding into the amniotic sac, so it's only carried out with the recommendation of the obstetrician. It often involves feelings of mild cramping for a short time afterwards, and carries about a one to two in 200 chance of further complications, such as leakage from the amniotic sac, infection and possible miscarriage. It's therefore usually only undertaken when the obstetrician thinks it's warranted. Given that Ruby was under 35 and all other signs were healthy, Dr Q recommended against an amnio in our case.

Confinement

What's happening to me

DISCARDING FAMILY VALUES

Month Five saw us crammed into Ruby's old bedroom below her parents' house, living out of a tiny wardrobe, in someone else's space. This was to be our home for Months Five, Six, Seven and Eight. I'd been apprehensive at first about living with the in-laws, but my feelings were unfounded as the Grandrubies made me as welcome as our confined circumstances would allow. The dog of course was in seventh heaven. She had twice as many people to dote on her.

In fact, it was Ruby who had to confront the demons of her past. Now a grown woman, she was sleeping where she had slept as a kid, but now with a man who was her husband and father of the child she was carrying. It was a bit like sleeping with a boyfriend while your parents knew about it, and then getting pregnant. How would Ruby cope?

As it turned out, she coped very well once she'd sorted out the differences in kitchen hygiene. This was focussed on the age of foodstuffs in the pantry.

'Look,' she said, holding up a jar of blackened coffee granules. 'Use by March 1998.' She threw it into the garbage. 'And look,' she said again, holding up a familiar black and yellow vegemite jar. 'Use by September 1997. That's four years ago.'

'We're a different generation,' protested Grandmaruby. 'We don't throw things away like you young people do.'

'But you haven't used it either,' said Ruby, extracting a bottle of tomato sauce from the cupboard. 'Use by January 1996.'

'There're so many preservatives in that stuff,' cried Grandmaruby, but to no avail. 'Either way it's toxic,' Ruby said, and she sent a tin of golden syrup rattling into the garbage bin. 'Use by October 1996.'

'Golden syrup lasts for ages,' said Grandmaruby. 'We used to live on that stuff. Not like the fancy things people eat nowadays.'

'Like Horlicks?' asked Ruby.

'Yes,' said her mother.

'I thought Horlicks was meant to be white,' said Ruby, holding aloft a jar of dry brown sludge like a TV attorney showing the smoking gun to the TV jury. 'Use by October 1992?'

'Well maybe that is a bit old,' said Grandmaruby, and flashed me an all-knowing maternal smile as the jar hurtled across the kitchen. I thought to myself, you're enjoying this, and wondered if Ruby realised it too. She probably did. That's how families relate, on the basis of games like this. Coded patterns of behaviour. Chiding as a compliment. Rubbishing as an expression of independence, but within acceptable limits, because no-one could really object to throwing out a four-year-old jar of jam, could they? A mother playing along with her daughter's fancy. I wondered what games would develop between me and M, and between M and Ruby. These things are latent in us, and mature over a lifetime of interaction. I'd have to see what M's personality was like before I learnt how to manipulate her(him), and vice versa. No doubt M would get the better of me. In bed that night I mentioned these thoughts to Ruby.

'Oh no, I reckon we've done enough soul-searching and got over our own parents. That won't affect us,' she declared.

'You think M won't learn which buttons she or he can press?' I asked.

'If you're level-headed about it, they should be mentally and emotionally healthy.'

'Can I quote you on that?' Ruby looked at me sceptically. Every parent I know gets driven to insanity by their kids at some stage. They all say kids test every ounce of your willpower. We'd be cool, she told me, and added in sugary tones, 'Besides, I think M will have a fantastic father. How could she have any problems with Daddy?'

'What about Mummy?' I asked.

'You tell me,' she replied, and puckered up for a smooch.

'I'll tell you this,' I said, ignoring the pucker and reaching under the bed. 'It's a gift to remind you of this conversation. I found it in the back of the cupboard. Chocolate Quick. Use by June 1985.'

PRACTISING PARENTHOOD WITH TIGER

Ruby needed the new station wagon for her work, so our plan was to head in early and beat the peak-hour traffic. The day's program was to leave at 6.00 am, go to the gym, shower there and head off to work. We also beat the evening peak-hour traffic by staying back late until it had diminished.

All of which kept a pregnant girl out of the house for thirteen to fourteen hours a day. It worked well the first day.

The Grandrubies had gone on a month's holiday and left us in charge of the house. We got up early and shut Tiger in the backyard, but when we returned later that evening there was no dog around. She'd forced her way through a hole in the fence, and befriended the neighbours. When we called she came pounding along the street with a smile that boasted of how clever she'd been.

'Tiger!' exclaimed Ruby with hugs and kisses. 'Aren't you a clever girl. Now Dad will have to fix the fence so you can't escape.' Even if it was 10.00 pm and pitch black. With a torch squeezed precariously between my knees I plunged my arms into the mass of spiderwebs and creepy crawlies that covered the ferns Tiger had squashed to get beneath the fence. Tiger leapt around the light eagerly sticking her nose into everything and getting frustratingly under foot. Sweating, hobbling over loose stones, I fetched a few logs of firewood from beside the house and dumped them over the hole. Tiger yelped as they hit the edge of her retreating nose.

'That'll teach you to be so clever,' I said, and slapped a spider – or something – on my neck as I dragged myself back to the house. Bloody dog. What happens when we have a kid as well?

Ruby rolled over sleepily beneath the sheets as I entered the room, covered in perspiration, splintery dirt and spiders guts. 'Did you fix it?' she murmured, but wasn't conscious of my reply. Which was probably just as well.

Up and out by 6.05 am, gym, work, home at 9.00 pm and Tiger came bounding down from the neighbours.

'Tiger! You got out again!' exclaimed Ruby again, stating the bleeding obvious. 'You're too clever for Dad, he'll have to fix the hole again.'

The dog had pulled the wood away, crushed the ferns and escaped. Holding the torch in my mouth, I floundered about the yard with bits of stone flagging to replace the wood. Tiger jumped around my feet. The spiderwebs and creepy crawlies stuck to the sweat on my arms. I dropped the torch. I dropped the stone. The dog yelped. I swore. Something bit me. I swore again, and slapped my neck. There was mush on my fingers – a squashed spider? I plugged the hole, and staggered to the bedroom wiping bug guts off my fingers.

'You must write the neighbours a note to thank them for looking after Tiger,' mumbled Ruby from beneath the covers. She wasn't conscious of my reply. Which was probably just as well.

Up and out by 6.10 am, gym, work, home at 9.00 pm, and yes, Tiger bounded over to meet us like it was a wonderful game. A row of stakes to replace the stones this time. I felt like one of the three little pigs trying to build a bigger house to keep out the big bad wolf. I squeezed the torch between my knees. I clutched the sledgehammer in my hand, a stake in my left. Mosquitos and other bugs buzzed around the light. I raised the sledgehammer. Tiger jumped. The torch fell. I brought my hand down. The sledgehammer crushed my finger. I yelped. Tiger jumped after the torch. I jumped after Tiger. The sledgehammer dropped. Tiger yelped and I squashed a caterpillar on the back of my neck. Bloody dog. I staggered to the bedroom wiping blood and bug guts off my fingers.

'You didn't hurt Tiger?' mumbled Ruby from the warmth of the bed. She didn't hear my reply. Which was probably just as well.

ALARM BELLS

Up and out by 6.15 am, straight to the gym, but before we got to the work bit Ruby said, 'I feel like I'm going to black out.' We skipped the exercise and went straight to work. She rang me at 10.00 am. 'I'm in a cab going home. I feel dreadful.' Not good, I thought. That evening I found Ruby and Tiger snuggled up in bed. There was a bucket on the floor.

'I just threw up,' said Ruby. 'I've been throwing up all day. I can't keep anything down. Take me to a GP.' I could see she was sick. I lifted her out of bed slowly and all but carried her to the car. Her shoulders were bowed, her eyes half-closed and her face was ashen. She leaned against me heavily as we walked into the doctor's surgery, where she sat shielding her eyes from the fluorescent lights. The GP surveyed her and carried out a barrage of tests. I was concerned. This was definitely not good.

'You're getting a virus,' he finally announced, 'and it will probably get worse before it gets better. I'll give you an injection of maxolon, and then it's off to bed for a few days.' Ruby looked up at him miserably.

'I'm scared about the baby. Will this affect it?'

'No, it's nothing to do with the pregnancy. It's viral.' replied the doctor.

'But I haven't kept a thing down all day. I don't want the baby to starve.'

'Babies are parasites,' replied the doctor. 'If there's not enough food in the placenta, it will start eating you.' He smiled. We looked at each other. Eating Ruby? In her state? 'The best thing you can do is go to bed and stay there till it passes.' I carried her to the car, to the house and to bed, where she slept.

Up and out by 6.20 am, to the gym, to work, leaving Ruby heavy in bed.

She phoned at 10.00 am. 'I rang Dr Q. He said get to hospital as quickly as I can, and get a drip into me. I've been vomiting so much I'm dehydrated. Susie (Ruby's sister) is coming around to take me down to Randwick. You don't need to come. He said there's nothing to worry about.'

Nothing to worry about? My wife and mother of my child is so dehydrated she has to be hospitalised? I cancelled my day and drove to the hospital to meet her, arriving there before she did. When I saw her my heart sank. She was in a wheelchair, her head in her hands, sobbing, green and sick. She didn't even register when I kissed her before she was wheeled into a room. A nurse said, 'I'll give you some time alone while I get the drip.'

'What's wrong?' I asked.

'She's badly dehydrated from the vomiting. She needs to rest.'

'Will it affect the baby?'

'Unlikely. It's the mother's problem. We'll get some food into her via the drip.' Then she was gone, leaving the curtain waving behind her. Ruby and I hugged.

'I'm so scared,' she said, and sobs choked her. 'I'm so glad you're here.' Another nurse came in, sympathetic and efficient. 'Are you conscious?' she asked.

'Yes,' Ruby replied.

'Do you know why you're here?'

'Cos I'm dehydrated,' said Ruby.

'Left- or right-handed?'

'Right.' The drip went into the left, plastic ID tag on wrist and ankle. I stroked Ruby's right hand and tried to tick the boxes on the medical history questionnaire the first nurse had given her. Ruby lay still with her eyes closed. 'I can hardly see,' she said. 'The room is spinning. Every time I turn my head I feel like throwing up, and I feel incredibly weak and heavy. I'm so worried about M.'

Another nurse took her temperature (high) and a blood pressure test (low). 'But not too much, I wouldn't worry,' she said.

'And the baby, will it be all right?' pleaded Ruby.

'I wouldn't worry. They're pretty hardy little creatures,' replied the nurse, and wheeled the machine out of the room. The first nurse returned. 'How are you feeling?' she asked. 'Better now I'm here,' said Ruby, not sounding any better.

'We've rung Dr Q. He'll probably get in this afternoon.'

'I'm just worried about the baby,' said Ruby.

'It should be okay. You've got a viral thing. We'll send in Someone from

...nity to check the heartbeat in about an hour's time.' Then she was gone.

Time in hospital is like an ugly surrealist painting. One hour is two, more even. It passes with mind-numbing tedium, in rooms with featureless grey walls, stultified by the heartless beat of monitors and drips and other indifferent machines. Hospital time is not measured in minutes or hours. It's measured in visits, by lunch orderlies, occasional nurses, less occasional doctors and maybe, the particular doctor you wanted.

There was little sound or visual stimulation. Just Ruby and the machine beside her bed, the drip tripping a little ring every second or so, grey vinyl chairs and a curtain. I held her hand. Every now and then she'd stir. 'I'm scared,' she'd say, 'for M.' Occasionally tears would spill over. Twice she rolled over to make herself comfortable and ended up dry retching into a bowl. Twice I rinsed it out and cleaned it, and sat down next to her bed. I went outside to the ward desk, and inquired when the Someone from Maternity might be coming to check on Ruby. I was told the call had been put in and she shouldn't be too far away. I asked them to check again. I didn't want to sound pushy, but it was my wife I was thinking of, and besides, it was a private hospital so I figured I could demand the service I was paying for. I went back to Ruby, to hospital time. 'Any news?' I told her there was none. I said that Someone from Maternity was supposed to be coming, but who knows when. Hospital time recommenced.

Eventually, after another hospital hour or so, Someone from Maternity arrived, wheeling a foetal heart monitor in front of her.

'Are you Someone from Maternity?' I asked.

'Yes,' she replied cheerily to Ruby. 'Look at you.' Ruby managed a grim smile. 'I'm really worried about the baby,' she said. 'I've been throwing up and I'm dizzy and sick and feverish. I need to know if the baby is okay.'

'We'll have a look then. This isn't an ultrasound, it's only a heartbeat monitor, so we'll see if the heart is okay.' She pulled Ruby's sheets back and exposed her tummy. She covered the Bump in translucent goo. She rolled the amplifier around Ruby's belly. We listened for the heartbeat we'd heard in Dr Q's chambers last month. Nothing. There was plenty of background crackle – Ruby's innards – but no heartbeat from M. Someone from Maternity smiled at us reassuringly. 'Sometimes they hide, and we can't pick it up.'

'Hide?' I asked. 'It can't go very far. Where can it hide?'

'Its heartbeat can be masked by the mother's,' Someone from Maternity replied. She kept on rolling the amplifier round and Ruby stared at the ceiling in despair. Still no heartbeat. Plenty of crackle, but no heart.

'Perhaps it's the machine,' Someone from Maternity said. She fiddled with the dials and knobs. Ruby and I held hands. Someone from Maternity applied more gel to Ruby's belly. We waited. Nothing. My heart began to sink. Where's M? Avoiding my gaze she tried again. Nothing. What was she doing? She smiled wanly, embarrassed by her failure. Where was the heartbeat? She pushed the monitor around Ruby's belly. Crackle. No heartbeat. I was getting tetchy.

'Is there a problem?' I asked. Someone from Maternity fiddled with her knobs, avoiding my gaze. She tried again. Nothing. What was she doing? Where was M? Suddenly Someone from Maternity decided it wasn't going to work, and with a nervous titter she packed up the equipment. 'I shouldn't worry,' she said, still cheerful. 'You can't always get it, but the baby should be okay. I shouldn't worry,' and she wheeled herself hastily out of the room.

We shouldn't worry? What the hell would she know? She couldn't detect the baby, let alone whether there was a problem. Why did she even come? What was her role in life? A brainless quack with broken heartbeat monitor. A hospital time marker. Useless. What the hell is going on? My wife – my pregnant wife – is unable to stand up or open her eyes, and they send us a moron with a dead machine. Where's Dr Q? We held hands and commiserated as hospital time enveloped us in its gruelling tedium. We would have to wait until Dr Q came.

'How are you feeling?' I occasionally asked Ruby, mainly to relieve the boredom because it was obvious how she felt. 'Disgusting,' she replied. Or foul. Or sick. The lunch orderly came with some dry sandwiches and cold soup for Ruby. She indicated I should have them. No sign of Dr Q. The lunch orderly came and took away the plates. We sat and stared at the grey walls. The dinner orderly came with a tepid chicken dish covered in a sweaty pink microwave cover. No sign of Dr Q. I went to check, anxious to obtain some information I could bring back to comfort Ruby. I was told they'd called his rooms. I was told he was in the hospital but they didn't know where.

'What do you mean you don't know where he is?' I tried not to sound impatient.

'He's here in the hospital, but we don't know where. He could be visiting his patients,' the nurse I was interrogating explained.

'One of his patients is in here,' I said, barely disguising my impatience.

'He knows you're here,' disguising hers far better. 'He'll be along as soon as he can.'

'As soon as he can,' I repeated to Ruby. That could be any time. We waited, and hospital time ground inexorably on. Ruby groaned occasionally. The drip dripped. I paced the room. The dinner orderly came and cleared away dinner. We held hands. The drip dripped.

Finally, the door thumped open and Dr Q appeared, pushing a small ultrasound in front of him. He wore the same reassuring smile he always did as he turned to Ruby. 'How are you feeling?' he asked. Wasn't it obvious? She listed the catalogue of horrors: last night, this morning, the failure of the Someone from Maternity, vomit, boredom and fear. Fear for herself, but mostly fear for M.

'Well let's have a look,' Dr Q said, and in fluid movements, hooked up the portable ultrasound, applied goo to Ruby's tummy and turned the machine on. 'It won't be as good as the first time, because this is just a machine I took from the maternity ward. I was just in the labour ward with a difficult delivery.' So he does deal with difficult ones, I thought, and was about to think how dare another pregnant woman hold up my wife, when the images of M flashed on to the screen. The same as before, but in less focus, her(his) little frame rolling about under the influence of Dr Q's detective work. I looked for signs of gender, but it was all too quick. 'The baby's as right as rain,' announced Dr Q. The TV image blackened as he removed the ultrasound from Ruby's belly. 'Perfectly healthy. You've nothing to worry about.'

'But I've been so sick,' said Ruby.

'It's a virus. A nasty one too, and you've been hit hard, but it won't affect the baby.'

'And the drugs I took?'

'They're fine,' he reassured her. 'If you can't keep anything down, we'll give you a suppository for the nausea, and injection of maxolon for the vomiting. Unfortunately we can't treat the disease, only the symptoms. You'll just have to rest until it passes. Get plenty of rest and stay on the drip.'

At least he left us reassured. We'd had a glimpse of M too, cocooned from all the traumas outside. I gave Ruby a tender hug, not too much because any movement hurt, and I left. What a day. Misery, fear, danger, boredom and a glimpse of M. To bed, I thought as I drove home.

BACK TO PARENTING PRACTICE

But it was not to be, as Tiger – out again – bounded up to me when I stepped from the car. With my eyes closed I got out the torch, some boards, more stakes and the sledgehammer, and fighting off a bounding dog, and buzzing insects wearily hammered together a fortress Taronga Zoo would have been proud of. I was tired, tired, tired. My head pounded, my eyes stung and my whole body ached. When I got to the bedroom, Tiger was curled up in a warm ball in the middle of the blankets. Maybe she said to me, did you fix it this time? Or just maybe, I thought as I shoved her to one side so I could fit into the bed, she said this is good practice for when M is born. Bloody dog.

THE SECOND ULTRASOUND

Up and out by 6.30 am, to the gym, to work. Raced over to the hospital after work just in time for the nineteen-week ultrasound. Ruby was already laid out with her tummy exposed when I entered the darkened ultrasound suite.

She gave a whoop of delight when she saw it was me. She seemed a little bit stronger. The sonographer was flicking switches and adjusting knobs like a pilot before a flight. She turned to me with a warm smile and explained, 'This one is more comprehensive than the first, because the foetus is more developed. We can do measurements of its organs, and check general health and development.' Then she turned back to the cockpit and flicked a few more switches. I wondered whether I should put my tray-table back and fasten my seatbelt when M flicked up on to the screen, a tumbling ball of silver bones with tiny eye sockets. Hello, M said, waving at us. Hello I replied, smiling and squeezing Ruby's hand. Then the baby flipped over and stopped for a measurement. 'A good heart,' said the sonographer. I could see the heart. Then M rolled over again. Look Dad I'm tumbling! she(he) cooed, and stopped for another measurement. 'Hemispheres,' said the sonographer. I could see the hemispheres. Then M tumbled again, and stopped. 'Kidneys are healthy,' said the sonographer. The kidneys I could not see. The screen was a mass of splintered charcoal. 'Where are they?' I asked.

'There and there,' as she indicated two indiscernible points on the screen. I was glad she knew what she was talking about. Same with the stomach, the spleen, the bowel and lungs. All healthy, yet totally invisible to me. I put my trust in the sonographer and squeezed Ruby's hand with pride and happiness.

THE SEX OF M

Then the sonographer asked 'Do you want to know the sex?' Everyone gets asked this question, and it's one of the more vexed issues in pregnancy. 'Are you going to find out what you're having?' A baby, as if we didn't know. What were they expecting – a rhinoceros? 'Do you know what sex it is?' A boy or a girl presumably, is there anything else? Most people I talked to didn't choose to find out, and of those who did it was usually the men who wanted to know more than the women. However, I did read somewhere that on the whole, most people actually do want to find out the sex of their little one early on, so obviously I don't talk to the right people. Whatever the case, a common reason for not finding out is a surprise argument. 'After all that labour I want to have the surprise at the end,' they say, including Ruby. I couldn't figure that. 'Where's the surprise there? It's either a boy or a girl. It would be more of a surprise if it had four legs and a horn.'

'But you don't have to go through labour,' she replied. She was right of course, thankfully.

The other choice was for me to find out the sex, and Ruby not to. But I knew that wouldn't work. I couldn't keep a secret, so if I found out the sex and she didn't, I'd give it away. So I left it to her to decide whether or not we found out the sex. And if we didn't, well, after all that labour, it would be – well we'd at least be certain of the outcome.

Then all of a sudden it was crunch time . . . 'Do you want to know the sex?' Ruby and I looked at each other and grinned. She knew I wanted to, and she wasn't really sure if she didn't want to. A decision had to be made. 'I'd like to,' I said, 'but if you don't, I won't.' Ruby hesitated for a moment, then nodded as much as her illness would allow. 'Let's see,' she said. Maybe my curiosity got the better of her.

So the sonographer poked around a bit, peering at the screen. She peered quite a bit in fact, and eventually said, 'Nope, can't see anything.' M's a girl, I thought. The sonographer said, 'That doesn't mean it's not a boy though. It's not always easy to see. It may be the wrong angle, or hidden, like behind the umbilical cord.'

Umbilical cord, I thought. That's not the umbilical cord! That's my son! But, the sonographer was trained to see these things. She could recognise a kidney in black pitch, so she should know. If she could see a kidney, she could see a willy. Especially a willy on my son if there was one to be seen. Ergo, it must be a daughter. 'That doesn't mean it's definitely a daughter,' the sonographer reiterated. 'It may be, but we can't guarantee it.'

M, the Maybe Girl, I thought, the No Guarantee Girl. Hmmm. The surprise was yet to come. We waited for the formal report of the ultrasound in the spare ultrasound room in the dark, because Ruby still found the light too hard to bear. She was a pitiful sight in her wheelchair and pyjamas, head bowed, pallid complexion. 'I'm feeling stronger,' she said. 'I haven't thrown up all day.' I brushed her hair aside and kissed her lightly on the cheek.

WORRYING NEWS

Dr Tubby, the same guy from six weeks ago, appeared in the shaft of light at the door. What news?

'All the organs are healthy. The heart, the brain and the lungs are all well developed, the kidneys and everything else are all growing well. All the limbs are the right length for a foetus of its age. In fact all aspects of your baby's growth seem healthy.'

Yay! I thought.

'There is one thing I do need to mention however . . .' said Dr Tubby.

What? I thought.

'. . . but before I do, I'll say it's nothing to worry about . . .'

Something to worry about?

'. . . even though you will worry about it . . .'

My child has something to worry about?

'. . . but there's really no need to worry.'

Now I'm worried. What is it?

'There are some tiny cysts on the ventricles that supply fluid to the brain. Not on the brain itself, but on the openings that the fluid around the brain comes from . . .'

Cysts? My baby has cysts on the brain?

'. . . but I stress it's nothing to worry about it. Your child shows every indication of normal healthy physical development. Only if it's associated with abnormalities in physical development would there be concern . . .'

What kind of concern?

'. . . if the cysts were associated with the deformities in the foetus it's likely that the baby would be . . .'

Would be what?

'. . .if not stillborn, then only live for a few hours after birth –'

Stillborn?

' – but I stress again, in your case there's nothing to worry about. There are no indications that there are any developmental problems at all, so don't worry. I know you will when

Then all of a sudden it was crunch time ... 'Do you want to know the sex?' Ruby and I looked at each other and grinned. She knew I wanted to, and she wasn't really sure if she didn't want to. A decision had to be made. 'I'd like to,' I said, 'but if you don't, I won't.' Ruby hesitated for a moment, then nodded as much as her illness would allow. 'Let's see,' she said.

you get home, but I'm telling you not to. We see these in about two per cent of cases, and by 34 weeks they're almost always gone. So if you want to have another ultrasound then you can, and most people do even though they don't need to. I know you will, but I'm telling you not to. About half of them disappear by that time, and if they don't, they don't affect the birth. About one per cent of people walk around with them in their brain without even knowing they have them. You could have some, I could have some. They don't affect your health. So don't worry . . .'

Don't worry!

'. . . they're just five millimetres in length and they'll most likely disappear . . .'

Five millimetres! That's huge! The kid's head is only three centimetres across. And you say don't worry?

'. . .so I'm telling you: don't worry. Okay? Do you have any questions?'

Like, what's going to happen? Ruby, as always, cut to the chase. 'So you think there's no risk to the baby?'

'None,' he replied. 'I'm telling you, don't worry. There are no signs of any need to be concerned. Don't worry. I've only told you because I have to nowadays. We like to give the client all the information.'

Determinedly not worrying, I wheeled Ruby along the corridors of the hospital as she shielded her eyes with the white envelope containing the ultrasound stills. Back in the room she climbed carefully on to her bed. I wasn't worrying. I kissed her on the lips and looked into her eyes. 'Are you okay with this?' I asked her. She nodded. 'Strangely enough I don't feel worried about it. Maybe I'm too tired, or maybe it's a shock thing which will wear off, but it doesn't feel like it. Maybe Dr Tubby just did a good "don't worry" job.'

'I feel the same,' I lied. Not worried. Besides, I told myself, everything else looked healthy, and we couldn't get the baby out to ask how it felt. We couldn't look into the future so we couldn't see what M would turn out like. Maybe it was one of those things that only recent technology has been able to detect. Dr Tubby said that lots of adults have them. We'd have to wait until M was born, and not worry about it until then. Not worry. See? Not worried.

'We'll have a look at 34 weeks,' said Ruby.

'Even though he told us not to.'

'But he said we would. So we will.'

'Are you sure you're okay?'

'Sure,' she replied. 'I'm tired. I'm sick. But I'm not worried.' I stayed a while longer. Not worried. Driving along the M2 I wondered is this what it's like to be a parent? Not knowing what to expect. Knowing the dangers, but powerless to do much about them. Just having to let your child do its thing. Sure, Dr Tubby said not to worry, but I was new at this, and wanted everything to be certain for M. That's all we ever really wanted. Certainty that she would come out all right. Or he. I realised I hadn't asked Dr Tubby about M's gender. If he'd seen a cyst five millimetres big, then he would've been able to see M's willy, if there was one. Surely. No worries.

Not unexpectedly, Tiger came bounding along from the neighbour's property when I called her. In my dazed state last night I'd staked out all the wrong places in the fence. The hole was gaping wide in the torch light, hemmed by a pungent fringe of squashed ferns. That was it. I rang our neighbours back home who kindly offered to take Tiger for the day tomorrow. Their dog Max and Tiger were great friends. Apparently Max had been missing Tiger, so they kindly agreed.

Up at about 6.00 am this time. Tiger looked at me with anticipation when I didn't lock her behind the gate, and jumped and hollered with delight when I called her to the car. I dropped her off at Bronte and drove to work. That afternoon I raced to David Jones and bought a whole new set of bed linen. We hadn't packed enough sheets for the four-month stint at the Grandrubies, and I'd been sleeping with Tiger for three nights. The bed stank of man and his best friend. A new set wouldn't go astray, in the short or long term, and I knew Ruby would appreciate it when she got home. My other best friend.

When I arrived at the hospital that evening Ruby was in much higher spirits. 'Yippee!' she yelled and raised herself up on one elbow. 'Give me a kiss. I've been so bored. I can't watch TV because it hurts my eyes. I can't read – there's nothing to do. But look, at least I'm off my drip. I went for a walk today too, just along the corridor. I had to hold on to the wall, but at least I got up. And I've had a wash, and washed my hair.'

BACK KICKIN'

'Dr Q said I could go home tomorrow. And look . . .' she said, whipping up her T-shirt top, 'I felt M kick today.' She rubbed her tummy. 'Not big. Like a butterfly, but I'm sure it's her or him. See if you can feel it.' She placed my hand on her abdomen and we lay still. I reached out with all my senses, almost willing for something to happen, but nothing did. I thought of M down in there, quietly brewing, turning and tumbling with inchoate life. My little M. 'No, she's not doing it now. They're only little kicks, so you might not be able to feel them yet. But you can feel them on the inside.' I looked up at her and grinned with pride. 'Now give me a kiss,' she said. A big kiss, tongue and all.' No doubt about it, Ruby was feeling better.

The next morning was a Saturday, and in daylight I was able to mend the fence properly. I left Tiger in the yard staring in bewilderment at the array of boards, iron bars, fencing and armoured plate that now blocked her way through. See if you can beat that, dog. At the hospital I walked Ruby to the car with slow, wobbly steps and drove home as smoothly as I could. She held her head in her hands as the world spun by and I had to carry her to bed. She brightened up at the sight of the new sheets, and snuggled under the cover. I put an old blanket over the top, and went to fetch Tiger who was standing for-lornly at the garden gate, tail hanging, whimpering at not being able to get at Ruby. Victory!

Now to explain to the neighbours why their fence looked like Alcatraz.

Ruby spent the next week in bed, attended by Tiger, her sister, two boisterous nephews and a nursing infant niece. A week of watching how a mother of three copes. I cooked meals and carried them down the spiral staircase to eat them in bed with her. By the end of the week she was up in the kitchen making toast, and professing to be ready for work. Her balance wasn't perfect, but it was sufficient to be up and about.

FATHERHOOD – A CAUTIONARY TALE

The run up to the end of Month Five exposed another issue about parenthood for me: being busy. Work suddenly exploded in the last week of March and the lead up to Easter. I was starting at 7.00 am, finishing at 10.00 pm, sometimes 1.00 am, running from meeting to meeting, totally out of control. This included weekends. Up at 6.00 am, kiss Ruby goodbye, drive to work, lift my head at about 10.00 pm and cab it home. Living on rushed lunches and late-night dinners. Only faintly conscious of a body next to me in the few hours I was in bed. 'Hang in there, honey,' I'd say, 'it'll get back to normal soon.' Thank God for the Grandrubies who'd returned from their holiday by then, and, in acts of extraordinary generosity, did our washing, and on too many occasions even made our bed. With their help and Ruby's patience I managed to keep Easter free. On Good Friday I was still in bed at 7.00 am, a sleep-in by comparison. Ruby lay next to me, her blue eyes open wide, staring at me.

'Hello stranger,' she said. I tried to draw her close. She was not relaxed. Nor was I. Gone was that air of soft intimacy. It'd been displaced by speed and stress.

'I don't mean to be a stranger,' I said and kissed her lightly on the cheek.

'I was worried in case it was me,' said Ruby. 'I wasn't sure whether you'd stopped loving me because I'm getting fat, or because I'd done something wrong.'

What can you say to that? An absolutely absurd piece of non-logic. I'd been busy for three weeks. That's all. And fat? She was pregnant, not fat. The 'big' issue again. Yes, the belly was getting bigger, but not fatter. Where do they get that from? And done something wrong? Why do beauty and guilt get so distorted? Of course she'd done nothing wrong. She was bearing my child, for goodness' sake, and she was worried about being unattractive and unappreciated? It was absurd.

Not that I said that. Instead, I laid it on. Thick. I fixed her with a gaze of absolute sincerity and said, 'Ruby, I love you. You know that. You are carrying my child. Even if you weren't I'd love you (etc.). It is I who has become a stranger, not you, simply and only because of work. I still love you (and always will etc.). I know you love me and I thank you (from the bottom of my devoted heart etc.) for patiently supporting me. I owe you everything (etc.). And no, you are not getting fat. You are growing our child, our baby (our future you and me etc.). You look all the more beautiful for it. And you have not done anything wrong (are incapable of doing anything wrong, in fact etc.). You are the perfect, the absolute personification of goodness and beauty (centre of my existence etc. etc.).

It worked. (It always works). She shivered, her eyelids fluttered and she drew close to me. 'Are you trying to get me to have sex with you?' she asked, eager with anticipation.

'Not trying, but I'll take advantage if it's offered,' I replied. She lifted her T-shirt and addressed her tummy. 'What do you think, M? Shall we give Dad a bit of nookie?'

I realised looking at Ruby's tummy that it had expanded over the month so that she was now visibly pregnant. She had a little bulge. I realised the sad truth that I'd lost contact with little M over the busy time. I'd not felt her kick. I hadn't seen her expand. I hadn't been part of the plan for her arrival. I hadn't kept up my reading. I'd become an absent father. Even though it was only a week or so, it wrenched. I didn't want to be an absent father, known for providing for his family materially without ever having time to engage with them. A new person was about to come into my life, someone who already exerted a powerful emotional pull on my attention. As I looked at Ruby's little bulge I wondered. What's been happening, little M? How big are you now? What do you look like?

What's happening to it

Month Five About 20 cm. TV remote control.

VITAL STATISTICS

Length: About 20 centimetres.

Weight: About 460 grams.

Brain: Still very smooth.

Eyes: Closed.

Ears / Hearing: Pretty much complete. It can hear things now – Mum's heartbeat, gurgling stomach, and the boompah-boompah, boompah-boompah of blood in the veins. It's time to get the Mozart records out, or AC/DC if you want a little head-banger. Alternatively you can sing to it.

Hair: The hair on the head and eyebrows is coarser than the lanugo. The *vernix caseosa* appears. This is a waxy covering, apparently held on by the lanugo. It offers protection against infection, a kind of waterproofing. It looks a bit like blue cheese and is most easily seen in *caesarean* births.

Limbs: Developing. Starts grabbing at things and begins kicking. Mother may feel the first kicks now.

Sex: The clitoris is formed. Everything is pretty much in place.

What's happening to her

Most women will feel the baby move in Month Five, if they haven't already. It's a special moment. Like the ultrasound, it's a very real reminder of the fact there's a baby inside.

The litany of ills may continue or she may be the picture of radiance.

As her body begins to enlarge, some of the later symptoms may begin to appear: swelling of the feet and ankles, a little stiffness of legs, maybe some cramping.

She's carrying a heavier load each day, and will tire more easily. This may lead to back-aches.

Emotionally, if she's radiant, she'll be on top of the world with occasional ditzyness. If not, listen to her emotions.

MORE ABOUT THE SECOND ULTRASOUND

It's common practice for a second ultrasound to take place in about week eighteen. It doesn't have to be precisely the eighteenth week, however. The purpose of the second ultrasound is essentially to get a better look at the development of the foetus (or in medical jargon, to make a foetal morphological assessment). At the time of the twelve-week ultrasound, many of the organs of the foetus are too small for the ultrasound equipment to pick up. By eighteen or so weeks, it's basically all there on display for the sharp-eyed sonographer.

They look at pretty much all aspects of the little one. Brain size, brain components, facial features (nose size, lips, mouth, distance between the eyes, etc.), spinal development, chest capacity, heart size, heartbeat, heart valves and chambers, blood flows and arterial construction, diaphragm, abdominal development, kidneys, spleen, stomach, bladder, legs, feet, toes, arms, hands, fingers, you name it. If it's there to see, it'll basically be picked up, ticked off as normal and noted on the report card for your obstetrician. So if there's a penis they'll see it, unless it's hidden behind the umbilical cord. They also examine placenta size and position, the volume of amniotic fluid, the umbilical cord (and its inner workings), the cervix and the position of the foetus in the wall of the uterus. And if they didn't figure it out on week twelve, they'll tell you if there are twins.

Mixed reactions

What's happening to me

COPPING AN EYEFUL

The end of the second trimester. Ruby looked pregnant. Noticeably pregnant, with a cute little mound poking over the top of her pants which she could no longer keep buttoned up. She would sit at dinner with the top button open, like an old geezer who'd had too much to eat, except it was before dinner. She would rub her little mound and say, 'Here you are, M, a bit of freedom.'

It was the kind of look where people were likely to guess correctly that she was pregnant. Earlier, they might have thought, 'She's putting on weight,' and discreetly not said anything. Now they asked, 'When are you due?' The earlier months are a risky time for observers. One sure way to cop an earful is to ask a woman if she's putting on weight when she's pregnant. Or worse, to ask a woman if she's pregnant when she's not.

Or even worse, to say, as a male acquaintance of Ruby's said to her, (and luckily I wasn't there at the time) 'Your breasts are getting bigger. Are you pregnant?' I mean, who's got his eye full of my wife's tits? And for long enough to notice a size difference? And not staring at her bulging belly? Keep your eyes on the road, sonny, your hands on the wheel. If you've seen one pair, move on and see the rest. Don't subject them to long-term scientific scrutiny.

Strangely, Ruby was not offended by the remark. In fact she was quite amused by it. 'It's nice to have a bit of cleavage,' she said. 'Something to flash around for you blokes to look at.'

Eh? What's happening here, I wondered. Back in Month Two when this kind of topic arose she almost bit my head off. Was this just pregnancy hormones, or something else? I couldn't fathom it: it was either sunshine or thunderstorms. You've got to learn when to pick your time.

More importantly, the bulge on Ruby's front was a not-so-gentle reminder that, yes, I was going to be a dad. Something for which I was responsible was going to appear. Six months pregnant is a bit like turning 40. You can see in both directions, past and future. You're a fair way there, and looking back, you've picked up a bit of experience along the way. But looking forward, there's a hell of a lot you still have to learn. There's a bit of time left, so you still have a chance to get it done, but not too much. And there's a glimpse of the end. The light at the end of the tunnel.

Somebody order some more tunnel, quick.

MAKING PROVISIONS

There was so much we had to do. We hadn't bought anything yet, apart from a new car and a new house. We had no pram (and is a pram different from a stroller?), no capsule (when do they need a capsule?), no cot (when do they need a cot?), no clothes (when do babies need clothes?), not even a name. So far we had amassed a couple of jumpsuits (jump? suits), an enormous bag for carrying loads of baby stuff, and a bread-making machine. I wasn't sure if the last item was a parenthood requirement, but seeing as we hadn't used it yet, like we hadn't used any of the other stuff, I assumed it was.

Ruby had begun reading books that provided lists of all the things we would need to buy. These included:

1 cot
1 pram
1 car
1 house
5 cotton shawls
5 woollen shawls
5 cot liners
10 woollen blankets
15 sleeping bag type things
20 singlets
20 T-shirts
20 jumpsuits
500 pairs of pants
50 million nappies

MAKING PROVISIONS WITH PIMPLES

To my mind this was appalling. I protested as much one evening, while I was admiring Ruby's naked profile as she peered into the bathroom mirror. Her growing belly, and her scientifically-scrutinised-larger-than-before breasts.

'M's only going to be about a foot long, and weigh about ten pounds,' I said. 'We don't need all that stuff. She won't know a nappy from a newspaper.' Ruby leaned closer to the mirror and put both of her thumbs on her left cheek. As she squeezed she said, 'So what're you going to do, wrap her in newspaper and put her in a shoebox?' She grimaced.

'What are you doing?' I asked.

'It's a pimple. Or at least I think it is. It's very deep, and it's swelling up my left cheek. Look,' she said, and turned towards me. 'My face is becoming pregnant too.' She pointed to a red mound on her left cheek just below her eye. Big belly, big boobs, big cheeks. Everything larger than – or with – life. She turned back to the mirror again. I continued, 'She won't know what she's in. If she's a she. Or even if he's a he. It's like my mother used to say, you can give kids the most expensive gifts in the world, and they'll still play in the sand with an old cigarette packet and some sticks.'

'So you'll be buying M a pack of cigarettes for her first birthday then. Ow.' Ruby grimaced as she pinched the pink mound. 'Besides, your mum is embroidering a beautiful baby blanket with roses. I don't think this is a pimple.'

'But why do they need so many of them?' I asked.

'Because they throw up and poo on them. I'm going to have to lance it.'

'What do you mean lance it?'

'It hurts too much. It's like my whole face is swelling up. Whenever I bend over it throbs. Where's the sewing kit?' She shuffled around through the old drawstring bags in the bathroom and pulled out a thin sewing needle. It glistened in the light.

'Yuck,' I said. 'How often do they do that?'

'Throw up?'

'Or poo.'

'Umpteen times a day.' Ruby leaned towards the mirror and put the needle point to her cheek.

'That's revolting,' I said.

'They do!' she protested.

'Not babies, what you're doing,' I said, at which she snorted.

'And besides, I'd get confused about what to put on. When to put on wool, when a jumpsuit, a T-shirt or a singlet, booties, gown and the rest.'

'Ow,' she said, put the needle down and squeezed again. 'Ow, ow.' A drop of creamy fluid emerged from where she'd pricked the swelling. She wiped it off with a tissue and said, 'You haven't had much experience with kids have you?'

'I was one once,' I replied. 'Shouldn't you stop that?'

'Have you ever changed a nappy?' she asked.

'Nope.' She raised the needle to her face. Even though I'd been a kid once, I couldn't remember when I wore nappies.

'Never?' Ruby was astounded.

'Will you stop that? It's making my stomach churn,' I said. She withdrew the needle and squeezed the pimple. 'It's not as bad as labour will be,' she said. 'So just get used to it. Never?'

'I've never had reason to. Mum changed mine, and ever since I was toilet-trained I've taken control of that department.'

Ruby reached into the bathroom cupboard for a bottle of creamy sludge. 'What's that now?' I asked.

'Facial cleanser,' she replied. 'Well, you have to learn now because you've got five or so years of it to come.'

'That's my point,' I said, 'I'll leave it until then. No need to start five years of faecal cleansing early.' Ruby stared at the mirror again. 'It's not working. I think I'll ask Q tomorrow afternoon before we go and see Brook.' Brook was a friend who'd just given birth to a son, Julian.

'Will Q know anything?' I asked. 'He's an obstetrician, not a face surgeon. Wrong end of the body.'

'He's a medico,' replied Ruby. 'I wouldn't want to be carrying something nasty when we visit Brook and Julian. I'm looking forward to seeing your first nappy change lesson.'

'On Julian?' I asked. She nodded. 'But he's only three days old,' I protested. 'Do you think a three-day mother is going to let a monster like me loose on her precious bub's bum?'

'It's for the cause,' said Ruby, 'to teach men how to nurture. And besides, on Day Three Brook will be absolutely knackered, desperate for someone to help her out.' I was incredulous. 'What, you get tired of this game after just three days? We have a lifetime of parenting ahead of us. It's not a long weekend in the mountains. It's a vocation!'

Ruby sauntered towards me with all her pregnant naked attractiveness and a look in her eye that suggested I was breakfast on wheels, boy, and I'd better start rolling. She put her arms around me and kissed me. I could see the angry swelling on her cheek. She looked up at me and whispered in a low and husky voice, 'You dear sweet earnest man. It was a weekend in the mountains that got us into this pickle. So best you learn the basics now, before the lifetime begins.' And with that the subject was closed. I was to meet my nemesis: my first nappy change. My first dirty baby's bum.

THE 'BIG' ISSUE AGAIN

When I met Ruby the following evening, she was looking glum. She'd been to Dr Q that afternoon. He'd told her the pimple was in fact a staph infection in a hair follicle. Ruby had initially feared Golden Staph, but no, Golden Staph was a different bug. This was just regular staph so nothing to worry about. And certainly nothing to concern M. Most of us carry staph around in our noses, according to Dr Q. Ruby probably got it when she was in hospital with the viral labyrinthitis. It's commonplace, and no, there was no need to worry about transferring it to others, not even Julian the newborn. A dose of keflex would fix it. I wondered did the doctors ever worry about anything? Dr Q never did. Dr Tubby wasn't worried about the cysts. Did nothing ever ruffle them?

'That sounds okay,' I said. 'It'll be gone soon, and you can still visit your friends. What's the problem, then?'

'Because it's official,' she replied. 'Dr Q acknowledged that I was having a rough pregnancy.' So, not ruffled, but realistic.

'Isn't that sort of comforting, hearing the truth from an expert?' I naively asked.

'Look at me,' she remonstrated. 'I'm fat, with big tits and an ugly face.' There it was again. The 'big' issue. You can't argue with it so I gave her a hug instead.

IT'S EASY AFTER ALL (NOT)

Brook, the new Mother, like a lot of Ruby's other friends, was a patient of Dr Q. That's how these guys get many of their referrals. If you deliver a healthy one for one woman, you're likely to be recommended to her friends. So Brook and the newcomer, Julian, were at the same hospital where Ruby had been with the viral labyrinthitis, and would be when The Day finally arrived. On the way there, I secretly prayed that little Julian would be asleep, or if not, at least clean.

When we arrived Brook was sitting smiling and cross-legged on her bed. I looked around frantically and was relieved to see a silent bundle of towels and black hair sleeping in the standard plastic hospital crib beside her. Phew, I thought. Why do we need a cot when babies can obviously sleep in plastic things like that? But all eyes were on the new mum. How was she?

'Oh I'm fine,' she declared, oblivious to the two tumescent red sacks beneath her bloodshot eyes. 'It's not too bad, I mean, sure, labour was painful, but in the end it's not that bad.'

So, labour's a doddle after all, I thought. That sounded positive. What about the kid?

'Oh, he's gorgeous, and an angel,' boasted the new mother. 'He's slept through both nights so far, so I really haven't had any ill effects. I've had some great sleep and I've been able to catch up on the birth. He's a peaceful little fellow.'

So, children are angels from heaven who sleep all the time. That sounded positive too. What about caring for him?

'It's just commonsense,' she announced. 'If he cries, you feed him. If he poos, you clean him. He doesn't have any other real needs. Just feed him and clean him. It's not rocket science. The rest of the time he just sleeps.'

Well that's that then, they're easy to clean, easy to feed, and sleep all the time. And best of all, I can leave it to commonsense when M arrives. No need to worry now about early lessons in nappy-changing and bottom-wiping. We could go home happy.

NEW GRANDPARENTS AGAIN

Later that week we visited my parents again. It'd been some time since we'd seen them, and they'd not been shown the stills from the nineteen-week ultrasound.

It was the same routine as last time. Mum seized the envelope containing the pictures and raced into the living room. Dad found himself trapped behind the screen door on the balcony as Mum aimed a barrage of enthusiastic questions at Ruby about the images. Dad finally fought his way in to peer over Mum's shoulder as she scrutinised the funny snowflake pictures. So intense was their focus that I could've said anything without provoking a response.

Me: 'The new car's going well.'
Mum: 'What's that there?'
Ruby: 'M's heart.'

Mum: 'It's little beating heart.'
Dad: 'A good heart.'
Me: 'I'm dying of cancer.'
Mum: 'What's that there?'
Ruby: 'M's liver.'
Mum: 'Her little liver?'
Dad: 'A good liver.'
Me: 'I'm giving up my job and going to Tibet to become a monk.'
Mum: 'And what's that?'
Ruby: 'M's spine.'
Mum: 'Isn't that cute – all those little bones.'
Dad: 'A good spine.'
Me: 'I'm going to sell M into slavery before she's one.'
Mum: 'Are those its arms?'
Ruby: 'Yes.'
Mum: 'Aren't they gorgeous little things?'
Dad: 'Good arms.'
Me: 'We're naming her Beetlegwerp.'
Mum: 'And is that her little head?'
Ruby: 'Yes.'
Mum: 'Hello, little one.'
Dad: 'A good head.'
Me: 'I'm the prince of an evil empire.'
Mum: 'Give me a look at your tummy.'
Me: 'Princes of evil empires don't show their tummies.'

'Not yours stupid,' said Mum, and Ruby lifted the front of her shirt to reveal the bulge of her pregnancy. Dad turned away in mock embarrassment and Mum placed a hand on Ruby's belly. 'Can you feel it kick?'

'Sometimes,' Ruby replied, 'but only little ones.' Mum paused for a moment with her hand gently placed on the stretched white expanse of skin, hoping for a sign of movement, but there was none.

Mum then took Ruby by the hand and led her into the bedroom. I tagged along behind. Mum lifted the cover on the bed and revealed, on the corner of a sheet, a small pink hand-embroidered rosebud. She glowed with pride. 'It's my practice one, before I do little M's blanket,' she explained. 'I'm making her a baby's blanket, with a ring of roses for her to lie on. And every time I get the needlework out I think: I'm doing this for my bub. I'm doing this for my bub.'

She glowed with happiness. My wonderful mum.

NAMING RIGHTS (AND WRONGS)

It was coming to the end of the second trimester. That meant we had three months left, and we hadn't seriously turned our minds to what we might call M when he or she was born. If truth be told, I'd been studiously avoiding the subject, because it's so incredibly difficult.

How on earth do you choose a name for your child? I had no idea where to start. The task was too daunting. But as it was well past halfway to The Day, I had to force myself to start thinking about it.

The first mistake I made was to buy some books, all of which boasted of an extraordinary number of names. *Over 1,000 Baby Names and Meanings*. That seemed okay, a rich source of possibilities. *3,500 Baby Names*. Okay 3,500 – a back up resource for the first 1,000. *5,000 Names for Babies*. 5,000? Isn't that a bit much? *11,000 Names for Australian Babies*. Eleven thousand, and only for Australian babies! *35,000++ Names for Your Child*. Help! I'm drowning in a sea of names!

The second mistake I made was to turn to the internet. There are numerous sites there, each of which had an infinite number of names on them. It seemed I'd never be able to find a name, and M would be left a mere letter. Heeeelp!

I closed the books and turned off the computer, and tried a different approach. I asked the question: Why do people name their children the way they do? What criteria drives their choice? When I thought about it, there are as many reasons for choosing names as there are names themselves:

Tradition – Charles, Elisabeth

After grandparents' names – Charles, Elisabeth

Because you're a royalist – Charles, Elisabeth

Because you're English – Charles, Elisabeth

Royalism with a twist – Chahls, Ellyzabethe

Biblical – David, Goliath

Hindu – Vishnu, Parvati

After famous people – Adolf, Marie-Antoinette

Fashion – Kylie, Prince

New Age – Sky, Rainbow Pool

Religion – Eve, Lucifer

Wacko – Jacko, George Bush.

Or, as my father asked one afternoon, 'So what will you call him when he arrives – something reliable like Ronald, or Christopher?'

Reliable? Where do you get that from? Is giving your kid a reliable name a reason for calling him that? And Ronald? Who would call their child Ronald nowadays? Reliable Ronald? And if it's a girl? Ronaldette and Christophene?

That's the approach one book took: to give names increased spin and make them more individual through tricks such as adding 'ene' at the end to feminise them like Davidene or Peterene (although I didn't see girls' names being masculinised – there were no Elisebs or Jenniferts). It also recommended misspelling names to individualise them like Davyd or Peyter (thereby burdening your child with a lifetime of spelling its name every time it meets someone new).

What meaning did I want to give my child, and why? Strength? Peacemaker? A fighter? Reliable? ... And even if I found a meaning, where would I find a name to match?

I decided other people's criteria weren't a reliable guide after all. So I made my own list:

- I like names that mean something. You invest your child with something which he or she can identify with throughout life.

- I didn't want fashionable names that just sound nice, because in ten years they might not. Basically, that meant any of the top ten names in the last ten years was out.

- I didn't really want to name M after a famous person because my Australian tall poppy instinct said that if you're famous you did something underhand to get there. For example, Joan of Arc was, on the one hand, a heroic medieval feminist, but on the other, she was a loony schizophrenic religious warmonger.

- The name had to sound right. Beetlegwerp might be medieval Gaelic for intelligent, handsome peacemaker, but he'd get killed in the playground (thus he'd have to be an intelligent, handsome peacemaker to survive).

I set out to follow these criteria, but fell apart immediately on the first item. What meaning did I want to give my child, and why? Strength? Peacemaker?

A fighter? Reliable? It was hopeless. And even if I found a meaning, where would I find a name to match? All the books had the wrong end of the stick. They started with the name, and then gave the meaning. I wanted a name that encapsulated love, peace, passion, wealth, health and wisdom, without actually naming my child Love Peace Passion Wealth Health Wisdom. I needed a thesaurus, not a naming book. At this point, I rang up Guru Dave. 'Help! I can't name our future child. How do you choose?'

'I have no idea. It's a bloody impossible task.'

'So how did you name your child?'

'I don't know. It just sounded nice. I liked the name. Good luck.' He hung up.

I rang my mother. 'Mum, how did you choose my name?'

She replied, 'I don't know. It just sounded nice. We liked the name. It was as good as any.'

'What does it mean?'

'I don't know.'

'Thanks Mum.'

'Good luck.'

Despondent, I returned to the name books again. The one I liked most was the *Penguin Dictionary of First Names*, because for each of the umpteen thousand names it contained, it gave the meaning, the history and famous (or infamous) previous owners. This was a comprehensive look at the problem. It was a bit of an eye-opener too. Some names aren't as attractive as you might think. For example, Deborah means bee, Calvin means bald, and Phillip, bless his cotton jocks, is a lover of horses. Sharon is a plain in Israel, Whitney a white island, and if your parents were cruel enough to call you Burleigh, you are a field filled with knotted trees. Must have been a bad hangover the night you were conceived.

Anyway, Ruby and I began drawing up lists. It would've been easier if we'd found out the sex because it would have cut the list in half. We would've had to look at only an infinity of names, not a double infinity. Another reason to find out the sex of the baby early on.

It's not an easy process at all, unless you're blessed with being fixated on a particular name. Some people have always wanted a boy named Ken, or a girl named Barbie. Why? Who knows. Probably something from their childhood. Ruby and I made a short list each, and painstakingly and politely rejected each other's suggestions, along with our own.

NAME – REASON FOR REJECTING IT

Millicent – Too Edwardian.

Patience – Too staid.

Margaret – Too old fashioned

Manfred – As in Manfred Mann's Earth Band? Never liked them.

Lena – It doesn't mean anything.

Africa – After the continent? You are kidding.

Aisha – Means 'alive', sounds nice, but I'm not Arabic.

Eloise – French names are good, but it means wide. She could get called barge-arse at school.

Heath – Is a bush.

Myra – From the Latin, meaning wonderful. Myra Hindley was a notorious murderer.

Miles – As in I can see for – ? Ummm, maybe. (Pause). Nope.

Tony – I knew a Tony at school who was a real dope.

Toni – Too close to dopey Tony.

You can see how easy it is not to pick a name. Try to actually decide on one. We struggled on without success.

I added another two names to my list and took them off again. I looked at the calendar. I figured we still had three months to work it out. I added two more names to the list and closed the books. I handed the list to Ruby and said, 'Tell me tomorrow they're no good.' She handed me hers. 'Ditto,' she said.

RECYCLING

Now that Ruby was showing, friends started showering her with hand-me-downs from their pregnancy wardrobes. Ruby collected shirts and skirts and tops and bottoms from all her friends who had themselves received them from others in the circle. 'Sandy gave me this,' Jill would say, 'but she won't mind if I give it to you.' And Sandy said, 'Try this, I got it from Jill, she won't mind.' In every case there was a feeling of relief to be rid of the clothes, partly because they'd never felt attractive in them, and partly as a declaration of intent: that they weren't going to have any more children.

Yael, a good friend who runs a fantastic cake manufacturing company called the Good Food Company, said come on out to the factory as she had lots of stuff stored there. So we went to her factory, and followed her to a back storeroom behind the fridges of chocolate cakes and mango and coconut sponges where she disappeared into a mountain of garbage bags. Yes, she'd been speaking the truth. She had a lot of stuff there. From deep within the mound of items, she hurled a barrage of hand-me-downs towards us. A bouncing bassinet. A pram. A coloured mat with suspended mobiles. A highchair. A cot. A bottle cleaner. Black garbage bags full of singlets, T-shirts, leggings, baby wraps, blankets, towels, clothes, nappies. All flying out from the far corners of the warehouse, into daylight for the first time in a couple of years. We gratefully filled the station wagon with the free loot. There was an awful lot of the stuff that was listed in the various baby books that Ruby had been reading. Perhaps this caper wasn't going to be too bad after all.

MOVEMENT AT THE STATION!

That night as we lay in bed exhausted from moving all the gear into storage at the Grandrubies, Ruby lifted her top to show me her stomach. 'Put your hand here,' she said and guided my hand to one side of her belly button. I waited. Nothing. Ruby held my hand still. I waited a little longer. Then I felt a little flicker beneath the skin. I almost sprang out of the bed with joy. That was M! My little M! Kicking around inside mum! How big was M now, I wondered. M! We have movement! I pulled myself close to Ruby's tummy, and watched intently for any signs. Holding my hand in place in case M moved. She(he) didn't, but she(he) had. That was the important – and amazing – thing. M had registered her(his) presence. I lay back on the pillow and gazed adoringly at Ruby. She looked back at me and said, 'You should have seen the look on your face.'

What's happening to it

VITAL STATISTICS

Length: About 25 centimetres.

Weight: About 920 grams.

Brain: Grooves start appearing on the brain so it looks more like the adult version.

Eyes: Closed for future use.

Ears / Hearing: Growing.

Hair: Lanugo, vernix.

Limbs: Growing.

Month Six About 25 cm. Hand drill.

What's happening to her

She's really showing now, a major Frontal Bulge on display. The baby inside will be bouncing around a lot more. If you haven't felt it during Month Five, you most likely will this month.

See the previous months for the other physical effects. Has morning sickness gone? Or got worse? How about leg cramps? Stiff back? Pins and needles? Her belly may be getting itchy too, as the skin stretches.

Or does she agree that she is the most beautiful creature around?

The nesting instinct – if that's the proper term – will begin to kick in. An increased focus on preparing the house, the child's room, her life generally and thoughts about the impending labour. Time to book into a childbirth class if you haven't done so already.

She may be increasingly clumsy towards the end of the second trimester. Her body is now bigger and her movements may be feeling a bit odd to her as she carries the extra weight around with her.

Sharper focus

What's happening to me

THE UNIFORM

The beginning of the third, and last, trimester. The road home. The beginning of the end. The last stretch. The final push, so to speak. Ruby was really showing now. She baulked at the ugliness of most maternity clothes, bought a wardrobe of clothes two sizes larger than her normal, and spent the weekends in a standard uniform of red leggings, joggers and a rugby top. For variation, she wore a polo neck jumper on colder days. She looked radiant, despite what she wore. It was as if the illnesses of the last six months had suddenly evaporated, and all the hormones of pregnancy had turned positive and life-producing. With her belly leading the way, she swaggered about the house like an old farmhand in a cattle yard – straight back, weight on her heels, arms slightly splayed and tummy hanging over the waistline of her pants.

INFORMATION OVERLOAD

The realisation that The Day was only three months away re-focussed our minds on what was about to happen to our lives. Or to be more truthful, it probably focussed my mind a bit more because Ruby had been more diligent than me in reading the growing library of books about pregnancy, pre-birth, birth, post-birth, post-post-birth and every other odd moment in between. Or to be even more truthful, I became more focussed on the birth process because Ruby began to nag me about it. 'You've got to read this book,' she'd say, 'it's got all the details about the hospital.' Or 'It'll tell you what I need.' Or what the nursery needs. Or the fifty zillion items of clothing and bedtime accessories the tiny neonate will need. Or the steps of labour. Or the problems of nipple rash while breastfeeding.

Was all this something I wanted to know about? Sure, I wanted to be sympathetic and supportive, but did I have to read all this stuff beforehand? The answer was probably yes, I could support her better if I knew a lot more of what she was going through. My difficulty was that, biologically, I was one step removed from it all. For the woman going through the process – with hormones and God knows what swilling around inside her brain – all this stuff is intensely meaningful. She knows that when the baby kicks she feels good, and when it doesn't she begins to wonder and worry. She thinks about the labour because her belly is swelling. She thinks about breastfeeding because her breasts are getting bigger. (Yep, they were still growing, even in Month Seven. I wondered when they would stop). It made sense that her observation of the pregnancy would be more intimate than my observation of her pregnancy. She was observing herself.

None of her physical stuff was happening to me, but something *was* definitely happening. My belly was undeniably getting bigger. I was suffering what many of my friends had suffered as their partners went through pregnancy: the sympathetic pregnancy. An increase in the father's waistline directly proportionate to the month of pregnancy.

It's almost impossible to avoid, especially in my case. At least that's my story. As Ruby grew larger she was less inclined to exercise and more inclined to sleep. We'd stopped trying to go to the gym in the morning after her stint in hospital with the viral labyrinthitis, and evenings were ruled out because she was too tired after a full day's work. Sure, there are some stories of madwomen who run marathons up until the day of labour (not if it's a hot day), but Ruby had decided to indulge herself in the last three months, particularly because the first six had been so traumatic.

This attitude, combined with Grandmaruby's cooking, did nothing to help my waistline. In keeping with her general philosophy of looking after the father-to-be, she was cooking up a storm. Every evening there was a full cooked dinner waiting for us when we got home: roast beef, or a chicken casserole, or pork chops or a lamb rack, followed by a sumptuous lemon delicious or chocolate pudding or upside-down cake. With cream. And ice-cream. A main course with pud – who lives in such luxury these days? Not to mention sommelier Grandparuby who was always armed with a bottle of red or two, some whisky or port afterwards and a picking of great cheese after the meal: stilton, brie, whatever. Not to mention the chocolate biscuits in the tin, the nuts in the cupboard, the Wagon Wheels in the fridge, the ice-cream in the freezer, the shortbread in the pantry and the cakes on the kitchen bench.

And it wasn't just food. Every luxury was made available. Our bed was made. Our laundry was done. Tiger was walked. Our clothes were ironed. We weren't allowed to lift a finger. I even had my handkerchiefs ironed. Can you believe it? This was livin'.

All we could do was lie back and enjoy it. Literally. Sunday mornings were especially bad, (or good, depending on your perspective). Each week we rented a stack of videos, and watched them in bed, consuming a lavish breakfast of fried eggs, bacon, and the works prepared by Chef Grandmaruby, or in the afternoons finishing off the chocolate-chip ice-cream from the night before.

So these factors – diet and exercise – led to my demise and expansion, at much the same rate as Ruby. Although it wasn't really the same thing. She was eating as much, but expanding the Frontal Bulge with a brewing baby. I was just brewing a fat gut, my sympathetic pregnancy.

All of which, if nothing else, leads me to my original point: the closest men can really come to experiencing pregnancy is by either looking at their partner or overeating. Otherwise we're on the outer. We are observers. I observed her tummy getting rounder. I observed her breasts getting larger. I could place my hands on her stomach and feel the kicks getting stronger. But I didn't have the same intimacy of the experience as Ruby. As a result, the information in the various books became information overload. When to feel what. What to buy when. Formula versus breast. Jumpsuits versus nappysacks. Those cramping feelings, too early for *Braxton Hicks* (see page 133). Too early for *contractions*. Practice Braxton Hicks. Practice phoney labour pains. It was all a confusion of facts and figures, relating to female bits and pieces. I had no internal chronology to structure my reading. No hormonal psychology to order my understanding.

None of her physical stuff was happening to me, but something was definitely happening. My belly was undeniably getting bigger. I was suffering what many of my friends had suffered as their partners went through pregnancy: the sympathetic pregnancy.

My own initial thoughts had been (without wanting to denigrate Ruby's concerns) the bigger picture. How I might provide for little M as she (he) grows up. What financial demands will arise. Health, education. Food on the table. How long Ruby could stay off work. How to juggle things like school holidays, personal needs, family demands and domestic obligations. When to plan for the second child assuming all went well with the first (we wanted at least two). These were all longer term planning issues which, because I was still tossing them about in my mind, I hadn't begun to discuss with Ruby. Some might say that it was a typical male way to behave: to avoid discussing unresolved matters, but to speak in terms of solutions and positions we have adopted. Whatever the case, I was frustrating Ruby by not addressing her concerns. When we finally managed to communicate we discovered an unexpected irony: while we had different lists of concerns in our minds, we had the same attitude to each other's lists.

'You've got to read this stuff,' Ruby said.

'I tried,' I replied, 'but I got confused with all the lists of things to buy.'

'Well learn it. I have to,' she said accusingly.

'But I don't need to,' I said, stupidly.

'Of course you need to. You're becoming a father in less than three month's time!' she said angrily.

'What do I need to know about breast pumps and cracked nipples?' I said, equally stupidly. 'I'm not breastfeeding.'

'So you can sympathise, and look after me.'

This was real pregnancy speak, the language of the need for protection. I had picked this up as The Day drew closer. Ruby's focus was narrowing upon the event and the immediate needs of the newborn for the first weeks after pregnancy. This was accompanied by a strong need for protection, security, comfort and the reassurance that she and her child would be safe and settled. Because I was the father, I was the one she most expected to provide this for her.

'I'll look after you, you know that,' I said. I tried to pull her to me but she pushed me away.

'You won't know how. You won't know what to do, or what's happening when I need your help,' she said.

'You'll let me know when it happens. You always say I'm good at picking up on what you want,' I replied.

'But there's so much to do. You haven't even changed a nappy.'

'I'll learn when the time comes.'

'And if we're bottle feeding, do you know how to prepare the bottle?'

'I'll find out.'

'And what's the best routine for feeding? What are the pros and cons of immunisation? What about day care? When does labour begin? What happens – ?'

'Stop! Stop!' I protested. 'It's all too much information. When I try to read it, it goes in one ear and out the other. I mean eye. In one eye and out my ear, or something. We will learn. I will learn. People have babies all the time, and they all say no matter how much you read it's always a matter of making it up as you go along. Every baby is different. There's time to get the basics in place, but if I push it all into my brain now I'll forget it, and get it all wrong. We can cross each bridge as we come to it.' She fixed me with an unforgiving gaze.

'You really don't care, do you.'

'Of course I care,' I retorted. 'I care a lot. My thoughts are full of you and M all the time.'

'Yeah, like what kind of thoughts?'

'Like how to provide for you, and for any sibling M might have. What our financial future might be. What schools they might go to. How to give them the best I can. How to adjust my life for your and her security.' That cooled her fire a bit, but she still had some spark left.

'But that's big picture stuff. Schools won't be for five years or so. We could be living anywhere by then. And a brother or sister will be at least two years away. Who knows what will be happening then. You've got a job, we've got a house. We have to focus on the here and now, the birth. All that other stuff – we can cross that bridge when we come to it –' She stopped as she suddenly realised what she'd said. I chuckled, and a reluctant smile broke across her face. 'Don't laugh!' she said.

'Listen to you,' I replied.

'You big ape,' she teased.

'Goofball,' I replied.

'I'm allowed to, I'm pregnant,' she said.

I'll pay that one every time. You can allow them everything when they're carrying your child.

ANOTHER CAUSE FOR WORRY

Still, there were basic things well worth knowing about straightaway. We'd booked in for the birthing classes next month and I was looking forward to those to pick up most of the information I would need as the basis of my preparation for The Day. One important piece of information was that the movement of the foetus is the best measure of its wellbeing. It's not just a delightful adjunct to pregnancy. 'I can tell M's well,' Ruby would say. 'She's been spinning around all day.' I would put my hands on her tummy and feel the little kicks as she (he) jumped around inside her (his) little capsule.

We had some friends whose baby had stopped moving about two weeks before full term. The mother had mentioned it to her obstetrician who examined her and basically said, 'You're going into hospital now, for an emergency caesar, and expect the worst.' The placenta had depleted, the baby had stopped growing and the only functions still operating normally were the brain and heart. There was a significant risk of deformity, developmental disability or even stillbirth. Fortunately, everything turned out just fine, and little Jordan is a happy two year old with more than the usual number of brain cells and a ferocious appetite for chocolate. But the lesson was important: by kicking inside the womb, the baby is actually communicating with the mother.

So, when Ruby remarked one Sunday that M had been moving far less, I told her to see Dr Q the next morning. Ruby replied, 'I think it's all right. I don't want to be a bother.' Where does this attitude come from, I wondered. Don't bother your doctor?

'That's what you're paying him for,' I said, laying down the law. 'M is half my child. I want you to see him. Tomorrow.' I would have rung him myself if she hadn't. She telephoned me late that morning and I could hear her holding back the tears. 'I went to Dr Q. He booked me into Prince of Wales straightaway, to get it checked out. I'm on my way there.'

'I'll meet you out there,' I said.

'You don't need to. Dr Q said it would be okay,' but the need in her voice was obvious. I remembered the last time she'd told me that I didn't need to go to the hospital: she ended up spending two weeks in bed with a savage virus. And besides, I thought, if the usually cool Dr Q says get to hospital now, it means something could be wrong. I told Ruby I'd be there, and grabbed a cab, trying not to expect the worst on the journey out to the hospital. All of a sudden I didn't want Dr Q to be ruffled.

When I arrived at the hospital I was directed to the maternity ward and shown to a room where Ruby lay on a bed, black foetal heart monitors strapped to her tummy like seatbelts. I looked at her and my heart lifted when I saw she was smiling.

'Hi,' she said, her eyes twinkling. She pointed to the bank of machines next to the bed, from which emanated the regular rowing sound we'd first heard in Dr Q's chambers back in Month Three. 'That's our little M,' said Ruby, and held out her arm for a hug. Much relieved, I leaned forward to respond and heard a huge crackling noise that almost ripped the machine apart. 'That's M again,' explained Ruby. 'She's having a big kick.' When I pulled back, the regular heartbeat of my child resumed: even-paced and foetal. I listened with joy and held Ruby's hand. The nurse entered and explained what the problem had been. Apparently M had turned around, so her (his) back was facing the outside world, her (his) front towards the rear of the uterus. M was still kicking just as much, but because the uterus has no sensation, Ruby hadn't felt the kick. When a foetus is facing the front, it kicks the abdominal wall, which does register sensation. That's how mother knows her baby is well – when it kicks her in the stomach. The nurse added that we'd done the right thing by coming into hospital to check it out.

FANTASIES OF THE DAY

My fears assuaged, I was able for the first time to take in my surroundings. There were timber veneer cupboards, a sparkling clean floor, a very comfortable bed which looked like it could twist and turn in any direction, and a bathroom to one side with a spa bath and shower. In one corner stood a maroon reclining chair. The whole room had an air of both hospital and home comfort.

It was, in fact, the delivery suite. The place where we'd be in three months time. As if reading my thoughts, Ruby said, 'This is the labour room. Look how the bed moves.' She manipulated the bed so that the end rose and dropped, the pillows fluffed and the bed lifted and fell. It looked like it did practically everything except shake the baby out. 'That's where they clean the baby,' she said, pointing to a small plastic bench beneath a light. Everything was neat and orderly. Everything was at the ready. I was surprised at how clean and efficient it looked, given what I understood to be the blood and mess that accompanied birth.

I had a vision of all this neatness suddenly being violently messed up with a kicking and straining mother, an anxious father, and a busy team of midwife, nurses and obstetrician cajoling a bloodied youngster out of a screaming mother. It seemed strange that these clean and quiet walls regularly echoed with the screams of labour, and these pristine floors and sheets were regularly soiled with the pain of birth and after-birth. Oh well, I thought, less than three months to go. I may as well get used to the idea. But I had my eye on the recliner in the corner of the room. It didn't show any signs of having been used for the birthing process. There were no stains or tears or dents. I decided it was the dad's chair, a place for him to rest while the cacophony of childbirth raged on around him. I saw myself in slippers, feet up on the couch, nonchalantly reading the paper while a team of medicos dragged my child into the world. I don't think so.

OTHER FANTASIES – THE SEX THING

The month of good food, a little wine, and relaxation, had done wonders for Ruby. She was looking fantastic. Her Frontal Bulge was as big as a football, and stuck out proudly for all to see. She happily showed it off to anyone who showed even the vaguest interest, lifting her top to reveal the bulbous white tummy that every now and then rippled and kicked with the signs of M's internal life. She glowed with the vitality of pregnancy. Even in her uniform leggings and polo neck jumper she looked sexy. At night she'd smile and cuddle up next to me in bed, and we'd talk about the future. What M might be like, if she was a he or a she, what we wanted for her or him, how we might manage as a family. Once when she was really warmed up she lifted up her jumper so her breasts spilled out and she thrust them forward. 'Look, for the first time in my life I have a cleavage worth showing off.' Then she turned around and patted her behind, and declared, 'My butt's not getting any bigger either.' I was about to point out her comments to the contrary on previous occasions when she said, 'This is great, I'm really enjoying it. Let's have sex.'

I needed no encouragement. Too many of my friends had warned me that these were the last days when we could indulge in uninterrupted lust together as our sex life would die after the birth of our baby. The Lord giveth and the Lord taketh away. 'You're too busy,' they all said, 'and too tired. Do it like crazy now, because you won't get it afterwards.'

Ruby furnished me with a hungry kiss and wriggled out of her leggings. She wasn't wasting any time. 'Take my jumper off,' she said and held her hands in the air, exposing her map of Tasmania beneath the Frontal Bulge. I obliged by pulling the jumper over her head and for a moment had a glimpse of just her body: her enlarged breasts, her round belly, her white thighs and calves standing on tippy-toes as I pulled up the jumper, her head an impression behind the woollen fabric. She jumped back on to the bed and stretched herself lustily, reaching for all four corners of the mattress. 'Look at me,' she said. I looked. 'Do you like what you see?' I liked. 'Do you want me?' I wanted. 'Take your clothes off.' I took my clothes off. 'Mmm, yum,' she said. 'Come and get me.' I went, like a starving man to a well-stocked pantry. I almost leapt on top of her and was about to kiss her fervently on the lips when she yelled, 'Stop!' I jumped back.

'What is it?'

'You're crushing M'. I looked at her: naked, enlarged, beautiful. 'You can't just lie on top of me or you'll squash M. You'll have to hold your tummy in.'

'I can't,' I replied, 'not after two months of Grandmaruby's cooking.'

'Well I can't hold mine in,' she said. She sat up, holding her knees to either side of her belly. 'Kiss me.'

'I'll reach over,' I said, and leaned over hesitantly to meet her puckered lips, none of our vital bits touching.

'Make love to me,' she whispered seductively.

'How?' I whined. 'I can't reach you.'

'I'll get on top then,' she replied, and moved to get up. But she was stuck. Her bigger shape had altered her centre of gravity. In the mornings she either had to lurch off the bed like a drunken sea lion rolling into the sea, or I had to help her up. On this occasion I took hold of her extended arms and hauled her up. Once off the bed the urgent long-distance kissing started up again, mouth to mouth, but not much else connecting. You could have driven a truck between us. I lay on the bed and giggled as I watched her attempts to clamber on top of me. On all fours, belly and breasts dangling beneath her, she shuffled sideways towards me, but got stuck trying to lift her legs over me. She turned over on to her bum and tried to walk crab-like towards me, this time losing her balance when she tried to get her arms across me. She tried to shuffle upwards from my feet, but overbalanced when her feet and hands collapsed halfway.

'You're meant to be more flexible when you're pregnant,' I said between hoots of laughter.

'But not for gymnastics like this,' she replied as she collapsed on to one side after another attempt. 'It's like having a watermelon strapped to my tummy,' and she hauled herself back off the bed for another go. Finally she managed to lumber herself into position – not with a moan of intense passion, but with a sigh of exhaustion and gratitude. The fates had finally allowed her to get this far. We took stock of the situation. Our bellies rose above us, preventing any closer embrace (any embrace at all, in fact), and almost totally obscuring any sight of each other. She supported her back on my raised knees, creating an angle of about 120 degrees between us. Not exactly the horizontal crush of love, but what could we do? It was the best we could think of.

'Hello over there,' I said.

'I'm exhausted,' she said, 'and we haven't even started yet. You don't expect me to move do you?'

'We could make it tantric and sit here for hours doing nothing,' I suggested.

'Ooh, M's kicking,' she said, and I observed her tummy bouncing with the blows of – what was it – M's legs, hands, something else?

'Don't look, M,' I said. 'It might put you off sex for life.'

'It's kind of funny doing it with M kicking around,' said Ruby.

'It's been kind of funny anyway, before she woke up,' I replied.

'I know, but it's like there's a third person here. I'm not sure I want to be doing it in front of our child.'

'I'm not sure we are actually doing it,' I said. 'And besides, it's not as if she's watching, or even knows what's going on. If she is a she.'

'I feel like a cup of tea.'

'What, now?'

'Why not?'

'Because we're having mad passionate sex,' I protested. 'Can't you tell?'

'No reason why we can't take a tea break. It's been pretty exhausting so far,' she said. 'Besides, I'm not sure I can get off you now.'

'What are you going to do, call your mother to make it, and bring it down? What's worse: doing it in front of your unborn child, or doing it in front of your parents?'

'Ugh,' she said. 'I saw them doing it once, when I was a kid. It really traumatised me. They were making such weird noises.'

'What, like – "Would you like a cup of tea, dear?" "No thanks I think I'll have an orgasm instead." That was how they did it in those days wasn't it? Did women have orgasms in those days? Or was that just a seventies invention?'

'Oh they had them, boyo,' said Ruby, and she wriggled a bit to rekindle my interest.

'Well then, cut to the chase,' I said, 'are we going to do this thing or have a cup of tea?'

So we did our best to dance the sacred jig of life. I thought of sea lions and dugongs, footballs and watermelons, cups of tea and not damaging the cradle of life strapped to Ruby's belly, as we smiled into each other's eyes from a distance. M was still kicking after it was all over. Heaven knows what she (he) thought about it all. It was only later that I checked up some of the pregnancy books to see if our method would have had any effects on the foetus. As it turned out we hadn't endangered M, but the books made for fun reading, and were full of advice on what you can and shouldn't do.

A LAST LOOK

The third ultrasound to check on the brain cysts took place later that week, even though both Dr Tubby and Dr Q had advised us not to bother. The cysts would have dissolved by then, they said. There were no signs of abnormality, they said. Don't worry, they said. But we went ahead anyway. We were first-time parents – we were entitled. And besides, it would be good to see little M one more time before the birth.

So we sat in the darkened studio as the sonographer gummied up the Bulge and cranked up the ultrasound equipment. The TV flickered and M appeared. Hi M! Hi Dad! Hi Mum! She (he) waved at us. I waved back.

'What are you doing?' asked Ruby. I pulled my hand down quickly. 'Nothing'.

'Were you waving?'

'No, of course not. I was just stretching,' I lied. Hi Dad! Hi sweetheart! M tumbled about the TV screen. Look at my bum Dad! Look at my hands! Look at my legs! Look! I looked, and wished I could hold her (him) there and then.

'It's pretty active,' I said to the sonographer, 'all that tumbling about.'

'That's me,' said the sonographer. 'I'm moving the sensor around to get a better look at various things. It only looks like it's the baby.' Oops. Silly me. 'But they are fairly active,' she added. 'You might see it kick.'

As if on cue, M shot a leg out. 'Ouch, I felt that!' said Ruby. Nice one M. Thanks Dad. I shot out a leg too.

'What are you doing?' asked Ruby. I pulled my leg back quickly. 'Nothing.'

'Were you kicking?'

'No. Of course not, I was just stretching.' Nice one Dad. Thanks M.

We waited for Dr Tubby in a side room. 'Good news,' he announced. 'The cysts have all cleared up, as expected. Everything about your baby looks healthy.'

Ruby hugged me close as we walked out. At the car she looked up at me with moist eyes. 'Our baby is okay,' she said, and buried her head in my chest. I hadn't realised she'd carried so much worry with her, and there I was kicking and waving my arms around in the ultrasound. 'Don't worry,' Dr Tubby had said. We were first-time parents. We were entitled.

What's happening to it

Month Seven   About 27–28 cm. Football.

VITAL STATISTICS

Length:	About 27–28 centimetres
Weight:	About 1.5 kilos.
Brain:	The brain is getting bigger with deeper grooves.
Eyes:	The eyes are open now. The foetus can detect light. While you're singing, put on the mirror ball.
Ears / Hearing:	The ears are growing unless you've been playing AC/DC very loud.
Hair:	Lanugo, vernix.
Limbs:	Growing.

What's happening to her

The third trimester – three long months to go. The novelty may be wearing off, and may take some of the radiance with it. The Frontal Bulge is becoming frustratingly and uncomfortably large. The kicks, mostly wonderful, can occasionally be surprisingly forceful if not downright painful.

Backaches are likely to occur as the belly expands. Some of the earlier symptoms may still be around. Her feet and legs may be swelling more. Her tummy itches. She may get haemorrhoids, or be short of breath. The symptoms may extend to sciatica: a painful pinching of the sciatic nerve down the buttocks and legs.

The larger tummy may make it difficult to rest in bed. If this leads to lack of sleep it can compound the fatigue and irritability.

You may see milk leaking from her breasts. This is called colostrum: the early form of baby's milk. The breasts (which, by the way, might *still* be getting bigger) are beginning to practise their productivity.

Emotionally, these developments can lead to fatigue, irritability, boredom and annoyance. The pregnancy is beginning to be hard work, and there are still two to three months to go (depending which end of Month Seven you are at). This makes nesting all the more urgent, and also increases the focus on the future child. It will bring to a head thoughts or fears about coping with the child and provoke serious planning on maternity, income, and how to balance domestic life, if you haven't begun that already.

The other strange thing is Braxton Hicks contractions. More common the closer she gets to full term, they may start at Month Seven (or occasionally even earlier). What are they? Fake contractions, as if the body is playing around with the idea of giving birth. The uterus tightens for about 20 to 30 seconds, and then relaxes. So, technically they are real contractions, but they are fake because they don't repeat. Real contractions repeat each other until the baby is pushed out (see The Day).

What's happening to me

ON DISPLAY

Two months to go. Ruby was looking very large. She was also looking very content, swaggering about the house in her leggings, proudly raising her jumper for all to see. 'You can see the kicks,' she would say, and sure enough her tummy would jerk, like there was something live inside her. Well, there was. It was funny. We lay in bed on the weekends digesting another gourmet breakfast courtesy of the Grandrubies and she'd lift the sheet. We would watch, and M would put on a show for us, kicking and rolling around like crazy. Ruby's stretched skin would bounce and bump in odd places as if M was pushing around inside to see which way led out. After a while M's movements would be swallowed up by waves of Ruby's laughter at the stranger inside her. I lay alongside and laughed and wondered at the miracle of the thing. This was something identifiably not Ruby inside her, unseen, but seen, unknown, but known, like a shy animal in a zoo display. We knew M was there but couldn't see him or her unless we waited. Waited a long time. Two months in fact, if all went to order.

BABY SCHOOL

Time to focus on The Day. Ruby had enrolled us in Baby School: two Saturdays of classes/tutorial/chats with nine other pregnant pairs run by a midwife. Some friends had done the series of weeknights, but we opted for two slabs of Saturdays because we thought weeknights would be too tiring. Ruby was still at work, trying to slow down, and by the time we returned to the Grandrubies in the evening it was a rapid three-course meal and straight to bed, leaving me to finish the port and stilton. Gee, life was tough.

So we were off to Baby School for the classes, to learn . . . to learn what? How to squeeze out a kid? Can anyone teach that? How to breathe? Friends said they don't teach that any more. To see videos of the birth? Maybe, but I'd seen videos of women giving birth before, and they weren't too bad. There wasn't that much gore or too many screams, so I figured they weren't showing us the whole story. All we saw of the caesar, for example, was the mother's head poking out from a layer of green sheets looking anguished. Oh well, if the videos at Baby School didn't show the whole thing, I'd find out in two months time.

CLOTH DOLLS AND HOSPITAL TALK

In the education room on Level 7 of Prince of Wales Hospital we were greeted by a table load of pamphlets on SIDS, Breastfeeding, Acoustic Research, Birth Booklets and a lump of crimson fabric and brown netting the size of a football. I looked more closely at this. The netting was a bag and inside was a stuffed felt foetus. This was a baby *in utero*, and the crimson folds at one end was the uterus itself. I recoiled with a mixture of horror and amazement. Was this felt stuffed thing on padded crimson material the best they could do? Talk about technology. Kids' dolls do better than that. They weep and cry and giggle and grow hair, but this thing was like something your grandmother in the country might have sent you for your birthday, if you were a girl. Surely they could be a bit more sophisticated. When you learn CPR at St John's you get a real live dummy – well half dummy and not live – but with textured skin, bone resistant to pressure and lungs that inflate with real elasticity. Almost real enough to introduce to your grandmother in the country. Not a cloth doll with puffy eyes.

'That's Gidget.' A woman emerged from a group of round tummies with nervous owners. She was the only one without a Bulge in front and a man behind, so I guessed she was running the class today. 'I'm Dorothy,' she said chirpily.

We wrote our names with black texta on white stickers and stuck them on our chests. I surveyed the room. Kitchen bench, a trolley full of instant coffee and hospital cakes. A video machine. Chairs in a circle. On the wall a poster of foetal development in saccharine cross section, the tranquil prenate almost smiling in its upside-down position, as it gradually moved from image to image down the birth canal. For some reason the narratives were in Italian.

There were nine other pairs of parents-to-be. Mothers-to-be beaming with pregnancy, fathers-to-be beaming with pride and not knowing quite what to do. I was reminded yet again that, for the first time in our lives, we men have no opportunity to be in control and this was primarily the women's thing. We can read up as much as they can, go to classes, buy the cots, pram and car, renovate the house, fit out the nest, but we cannot produce the child. In the group it seemed the women were chatting more than the men, comparing pregnancies and Bulges, illnesses and health. Who'd read what, what a friend had done, what they might do on The Day.

MEN'S TALK

The men for the most part looked lovingly at their women, validating their woman's experience. Yes, she'd done that, we found that best for her, she hadn't been too sick. What had we done, I wondered? Got them pregnant, yes, but you don't actually talk about the moment, if you're lucky enough to know when. About how we'd helped. But all there is on that topic is: whatever she wants, do it, be it a new car or cheese on toast.

But yes, there was one thing we shared: how we'd all suffered, in our own way, as partners to the child bearers. How we'd all had to bear the brunt of the first trimester blues, renovation demands, strange requests and Frontal Bulge Fatigue. Oh sure, it might not be as much as she'd endured or would still have to endure, but we had, in our own way, carried the flag for her and ourselves – made her breakfast in bed (well, some of us, but I didn't let on about the Grandrubies' hospitality), swept the floors, built the carport, scrubbed the car seat, not gone to the golf, turned off the TV, passed up the pub, got this, done that, catered to every little whim and fancy without thanks, as if it were all now our vocation, nothing more than we should be doing and really nothing in comparison with what she was going to do. Even flowers every Friday were expected, not a surprise.

DOUBLE TAKE

Having bolstered our mutual sense of self worth, we went to sit down as Dorothy called us to order. I saw Ruby in a corner and went to join her, but to my surprise there was a man there already. He smiled at me. 'No, mate, yours is over there.' I turned and saw Ruby sitting beneath the video stand and looked again at the woman I'd first thought was my wife. 'Hi, I'm Ruby,' she said. I couldn't believe my eyes or my ears. Here was a woman who looked almost identical to Ruby – my Ruby – in the same room. Same hair colour, same skin, same Frontal Bulge and same name. 'When are you due?' I asked. It turned out she was due the day before M. Sudden panic seized me. What if there was a mix-up at the hospital, and our babies were inadvertently swapped? Us bringing up someone else's baby, and our baby being raised by the wrong parents, only to find out in 21 years time she should have been with us. I looked the duplicate Ruby up and down. I hoped they were fabulously rich.

WHO'S WHO IN THE ZOO

I sat next to the real Ruby in a circle of ten couples all holding hands, with name tags and bellies on display. I wondered how many of the couples here would still be together in ten years, how many of the little unborns in these round tummies would still see the same parents in twenty years time. I wondered why I was having such morbid thoughts when I realised it was our turn to introduce ourselves to the group, along with our obstetrician's name and a due date. I let Ruby do the talking. Why the obstetrician's name? Does knowing that teach you how to push it out? The others in the group were:

Mr & Mrs Jymfit who lay on the floor doing their nine-month stretch and massage program, due in six weeks;

Seamus Fearwoman and his wife Gay who was evidently terrified of the whole thing, due in three weeks;

The Faux-Rubies, whose husband thankfully had a different name from me so I could at least tell him apart, due the day before M;

Mary Tightshirt and professional husband, who had it all planned out perfectly, due in four weeks two days and sixteen hours;

Dave and Suzy Goodtime whose pregnancy had been a hoot, hadn't it honey, except for the vomiting, due in five weeks;

Mr and Mrs Finetone who'd had the perfect pregnancy, suffering nothing but the envy of other pregnant women, due in two weeks;

Tom and Viv Hardnight who sat on top of each other, eagerly awaiting their child in three weeks;

Mrs Happytalk who wanted to know everything at once and her husband Adam who stared at the ground solemnly without moving, due in four weeks; and lastly

Gloria Sunbody who you wouldn't know was ready to drop in three weeks time if her hubby hadn't beamed so much at her Bulge.

And of course Dorothy.

A few things I noted before the main order of the day started:

- We were all married. Was this a plan of the Hospital, to put all the weds in one class and unweds in another? Or just circumstance?

- True to the literature, people's experience of pregnancy covered the spectrum from blissful health, to swollen feet and vomiting, to abject fear.

- No one else had Dr Q as their obstetrician. Did that mean anything? Was he an outcast? Were people avoiding him? Or was he an unknown genius? I decided it meant nothing.

Dorothy gave us all a meaningful smile and introduced herself and the course. She had been a midwife for twenty years, was now only part-time etc. Started doing these classes eighteen months ago etc. Safe hands, I thought. She's telling us we are in safe hands. And she was telling the women to sit on the floor, or kneel, or lie down or whatever feels comfortable, like doing the splits as Mrs Jymfit seemed to enjoy. I thought if she kept it up much longer she might drop the baby then and there.

THE FIRST TOPIC: LABOUR

And so to the first order of the day. A shimmer of apprehension passed through us all. Labour. That was the main topic – what we were here for. The inevitability of The Day. The process of pushing out a kid. Good pregnancy or bad, none of us knew what was ahead.

What is labour? It's the whole shebang, from initial contractions to cutting the cord. Or, in the eyes of most mothers, Hell with your legs open. Here's what I gleaned from Dorothy about labour.

First of all, there are two main stages of labour: *dilation* of the cervix, and the pushing or delivery stage. There is a third stage which is comparatively less arduous, being the delivery of the placenta (see below), although Dr Q did tell me that a lot of complications can arise at that point.

DILATION

Dilation is the longer stage. The cervix has to go from zero to ten centimetres wide to fit the baby's head through, which is a long and painful process. The pushing stage hurts but is comparatively (and I use that word advisedly) short, and has the incentive of light at the end of the tunnel (figuratively for the mother, literally for the kid).

Dorothy started at the beginning. The Italian wall charts came down. 'These have the best pictures, that's why we use them,' she explained. Can't Australians draw? I wondered.

The baby is inside and ready to go, upside-down now, head basically in the *posterior position* (facing mum's front, the baby's back to mum's back). The cervix is closed. There's a pocket of amniotic fluid beneath the baby's head – the *waters* – which will usually break at some part of the process. Nine months have passed. Time to go, says mum to bub, or bub to mum. Time to reclaim my body. Time to meet the world.

THE 'SHOW', AND THE BREAKING OF THE 'WATERS'

The first thing to go is the mucous plug which holds the cervix shut. This is known as the *show*, a greeny-brown slug of stuff, sometimes with blood. When does this occur? 'Anytime,' said Dorothy. 'For some women it's weeks before, for others it's the morning of labour. Some women don't even notice it.' Well, that's clear.

Next the waters break. That's the amniotic sac tearing and the fluid escaping down the newly opened cervix. When does this occur? 'Anytime,' said Dorothy. 'For some women weeks before, for others it's the morning of labour, or during labour. Sometimes they don't break, and the baby comes out in the sac, but that's extremely rare.' Well, that's clear.

Sometime around (or even before) the first stage, dilation starts on the painful road to ten centimetres. Why ten centimetres? That's the average head-size of a mature foetus. That's nature's way of dealing with us as bubs.

We really aren't fully developed when we're born, and we probably have to get out at this time because otherwise our heads would be too big to pass through a mother's pelvis. You might ask why *homo female sapiens* didn't evolve bigger pelvises. Yes, you might ask that. I wouldn't have a clue.

A question came into my mind. 'Dorothy, how do you measure the dilation?'

'The midwife puts her fingers or hand inside the mother,' she replied matter-of-factly. Oh God, I thought. Ten centimetres. More than a hand-span. This is not for the squeamish.

CONTRACTIONS

Dilation – indeed all of labour – is driven by contractions. Contractions are just that: the uterus contracting. It's as if it's had enough of this big thing inside it, and wants it out. So it squeezes. And when it does, it opens the cervix, teeny bit by teeny bit, mostly by using the baby's head as a battering ram. The kid is being pushed out, rammed through a tiny opening like a sledgehammer through a keyhole, bang bang bang bang . . .

Here's kind of how it works as told by Dorothy:

0 cm to 3 cm: The early contractions start softly, 'They're like period pains,' said Dorothy, and the men nodded sagely. In fact contractions don't usually seem that serious for the first three centimetres (although this can vary from mother to mother). 'You don't need to go to the hospital at that stage. Just make sure everything is packed, relax (especially the mother) and prepare for the forthcoming day (night, day and night, days etc.).'

3 cm to 7 cm: For most women labour will be in full swing by three centimetres, and most women should be at the hospital by then or wherever it is junior is meant to emerge. Contractions pick up from three centimetres onwards, and get a real rhythm going. On average they might be one every three or four minutes. And they are much more painful than period pains (and the men nodded sagely). That's when the mother needs to embark upon techniques of pain management: visualisation, active relaxation between contractions, massage, hot showers or baths, gas and maybe other drugs.

7 cm to 10 cm: This is real pain and effort. Contractions come every half a minute with not much rest in between. The body is straining. Mother is losing strength, losing control, hanging on. The last few centimetres are known as the 'transition', being the transition from your first stage of labour to the second.

Here it became apparent that there's a hotbed of dispute about childbirth. Dorothy said that at about the seven- to ten-centimetre mark, the mother will be pressured to use all sorts of drugs, to have an epidural, to have an *episiotomy* or whatever. Dorothy was from the natural process school. 'If you've got to ten centimetres without drugs then I suggest you consider seeing if you can go the rest of the way. Ten centimetres is the main effort. It's usually only about one to two hours left after that, and you'll have much more control of the second stage.'

So there are many schools: the epidural school, the surgical process school, the anti-medical home delivery school, the take it as it comes school, the rely on the professionals school. But here's a professional telling us to be wary of professionals. Others of opposing schools would criticise her position. Who do you believe? 'Rely on your own instincts and how you feel,' said Dorothy, and the men nodded sagely. How on earth can you rely upon instincts when you have no idea what's happening? The mother has possibly been going for ten hours just to get to the second phase, and has one or two hours left when she'll have to push like hell. Unless she's a professional triathlete she'll never have been that physically involved before. She'll be in great pain, the father trying his best to help her without really understanding what it's like, the baby may be stressed, and on top of that, we've never been there before. This is a totally new experience for us. Most parents-to-be have experienced enough to have a feel for most things: the pain of keeping fit, how to play games (in sport or business), how to do your job, how to be wary of politicians, but this is totally, totally new. Totally unlike anything you've ever done before. I book-marked confusion in my mind, not knowing how to solve the issue, or if Dorothy would be able to assist. Back to labour . . .

DELIVERY

Stage Two of labour begins after the cervix has dilated to the regulation ten centimetres. This is known as the active phase. (As if the mother has been lying passively on the bed for the last twelve hours). Contractions are still happening, but if the mother wants the baby out (if!) she has to actively push. With all her might, *and* in time with the contractions, *and* accompanied by strong urges to bear down.

One thing we can see now is the crown of the baby's head. The midwife can spread the vaginal opening wide enough to see a few centimetres of the baby's scalp, the first glimpse of the life struggling to get out. This is called *crowning*. I can't think why. More pushing pushing straining groaning pushing follows, until finally, slowly, painfully pushing pushing (aarrgghh!) . . . the head appears, sticking out from the mother's vagina like a grubby kid from a cubby hole. This is the moment of birth. Followed by the body on a second push. The baby is born. Champagne! Fireworks! Tears! Hooray!

But wait, there's more. The placenta is yet to come. If left to nature, this follows about half an hour later, more or less. These days doctors give the mother a shot of syntocinon which all the books say causes them to push it out straightaway (but which Dr Q told me is actually effective in preventing haemorrhaging). The obstetrician inspects the placenta, cuts the cord (with dad's help) and that's it. Contractions slow to nothing. Mother and child lie together exhausted. The baby is born.

'How long does all that usually take?' I asked.

'Usually about twelve to twenty hours,' said Dorothy, 'sometimes more, sometimes less.'

There are no rules in this game it seems. The show comes, whenever, if it comes. The waters break, whenever, if they break. Contractions come, that's certain, and they will hurt, but for how long is anybody's guess, and for each woman to experience.

I looked around. Mrs Jymfit next to me had twisted herself into a position where she could have seen her child coming down the birth canal. Gay Fearwarden was ashen. The Firetones beamed expectantly and Adam Happytalk stared solemnly at the floor.

That took care of the basics. What next, I thought.

THE ROLE OF THE SUPPORT PERSON.

The Support Person. That's us. The all important SPs. We aren't fathers, husbands, partners, lovers, men, any more. We are support persons. I liked it. I had a new social moniker. 'Hi,' I would say when I met people at parties from now on, 'I am Ruby's support person.' Obviously this segment was intended to remind us of our significance. We weren't going to sit here and listen to girlie talk all day. We were SPs. The other father Faux-Ruby looked up. 'That's us,' he declared. The men nodded. Dorothy began.

'The role of the Support Person,' said Dorothy, 'is to support the mother during labour and delivery.' Well, that's got that sussed. All we needed to know, really. Help out, pull out the kid, cut the cord and go home. God knows why you need the midwife or an obstetrician when we do it all. Probably as a back-up just in case we come across something we haven't experienced before. Like the whole thing. How do we support?

Dorothy distributed textas and large sheets of butcher's paper for us to work on in a group. The women were to tell us what they thought they might like. SPs were to list how they might help. The lists included:

- massages;
- encouraging words;
- food;
- massages;
- hot showers;
- clean clothes;
- massages;
- music;
- candles;
- perfumes;
- massages;
- a bloody expensive present at the end;
- massages, and not the kind where you stop at the breasts;
- alcohol;
- to be there;
- massages.

Well that was pretty clear. Labour involves a lot of pain intermingled with massages, and for some, perfumed music. With a bloody great present at the end. During a massage.

I could see the hospital was trying to make us feel significant in this process, and I appreciated their good intentions. But at bottom I knew the absolute first priority was the mother and child, and both would benefit from assistance by those with experience in the process: the midwives and obstetricians. But

Dorothy was sowing seeds of doubt in our minds about the professionals. The many schools of thought about childbirth reared their ugly heads again – the interventionists, the home birthers, the epiduralians – and it was our responsibility to choose the path we wanted to take. This sounded like the self-empowerment school and smelled to me of the blind leading the blind. That might sound rude, but Ruby had openly acknowledged that, despite all her reading, she knew nothing about what to expect. And besides, hadn't Dorothy just finished explaining the uniqueness of each birth? As for me, I had no hope. At least Ruby had a few internal indicators to help decision-making on The Day – the pain for a start – but how could I know what was best in any situation? Especially if Ruby was in so much pain that she wasn't able to think clearly or register her needs.

The Support Person. That's us. The all important SPs. We aren't fathers, husbands, partners, lovers, men, any more. We are support persons. I liked it. I had a new social moniker. 'Hi', I would say when I met people at parties from now on, 'I am Ruby's support person.'

I understood from the morning's session that The Day was a time when I needed to be 110 per cent calm, 110 per cent alert to her feelings, 110 per cent listening to her needs, and as clear-thinking as I could be to try to understand what might need to be done, and when. For example, when to intervene with an epidural, or when to hold the gas, or where and when to massage, what to say. Could I do it? I didn't think so. All I knew was the certainty of the birth. M would appear, come hell or high water, with or without me, with or without medical support, pain relief or massages. The thing was for me to maximise my role in the team that was bringing our baby into the world.

I looked around the room wondering what the other SPs were thinking. Mixed faces of doubt and concern. Adam stared solemnly at the floor.

STRETCHING THE TRUTH

Then Dorothy threw a grenade into the midst of my confusion. She casually announced, 'One way the Support Person can really assist the mother is to help her stretch her vagina.'

Did I hear her say that? Help stretch her what? Her . . . vagina? I glanced around. A circle of stunned faces stared mutely back at her. Even Adam

Happytalk looked up for a brief moment. Dorothy continued.

'The mother's vagina needs to reach at least ten centimetres for the baby's head to come out. Most women don't have vaginas that big (Most? I thought. Show me one who has and we'll put it on a pedestal). And most women have never had to stretch that far before now. So it can assist the mother if she begins stretching the opening before birth begins, to help the vagina get a bit more used to being that wide. To do this you need to massage the perineum a lot, gradually stretching it wider, to get it used to opening. The mother can do it, but it's easier for the man to see what's going on, particularly as the mother will find it more and more difficult to get her hands down there the more pregnant she becomes. Plus it helps the man get more involved in the pregnancy. And you should start as soon as possible, so that the area is used to being stretched by the time you get to the delivery suite. Do it for about ten or fifteen minutes a day, and you'll find it helps a lot on the day.'

She was for real, I thought. She really means what she's saying. I was to get down on my hands and knees before Ruby's open thighs, and place each thumb in the centre of her perineum just below her vagina, and push, stretching it outwards, making it bigger and bigger. Like it was a lump of playdough and we were stretching it out to make . . . well, to make a baby. I couldn't fathom it. It wasn't as if I was being asked to do anything normal here. It wasn't like stretching a hamstring after a run in the park. This was the perineum for goodness' sake, the delicate little area of skin between the female front and back. Not a piece of tired elastic. I'd been down there plenty of times before, but not for this sort of caper. She was making it sound like a remedy for health and long life. 'Do this every day for ten or fifteen minutes and you'll add fifteen years to your life and your vagina won't tear in childbirth.' The type of thing you could make an infomercial about. 'I've been stretching my vagina for ten weeks now and I've lost 45 kilograms.' Try as I might, I simply couldn't get my head around the blunt practicality of it. 'Just lie back with a cup of tea dear, and I'll stretch your vagina a bit.'

I looked down at the carpet. Everybody else did too. Maybe Adam had something after all. What on earth could be next?

BIRTHING POSITIONS

Next up, birthing positions. What the mother might find helpful on The Day. Basically it was anything and everything. On hands and knees. Standing. Hanging on to their SPs. Lying down. Sitting up. Kneeling with head on chair. Walking around. On a trapeze. On a tight rope. Swinging from the chandelier. Parachuting. Basically whatever gets the bub out quickest.

Then pain relief. The virtues of gas, pethidine, epidural, caesarean. Medical stuff. Try it. Don't try a caesar if you can avoid it though. In strength of relief it goes:

1. screaming;
2. squeezing SP's arm (neck/testicles/etc.) till he blacks out;
3. gas;
4. kneeing SP in the balls for getting her in this mess;
5. pethidine;
6. epidural (a spinal block which knocks out feeling in her body, from the waist down);
7. caesar.

We got to see some videos at this point. A natural birth unassisted by drugs. A woman using gas. An epidural. A caesar. None of them showed the real gory bits though. Perhaps there weren't any. We didn't see a needle going into the spine. We didn't see the cut of the caesar or the blood pool opening of the womb. No cut for the episiotomy, and no stitches. No *forceps*. We saw the mother smiling nervously at her SP over the green sheets.

We saw the mother groaning on the gas, taking showers, kneeling and grimacing with pain. We saw the moment of birth, too. The greasy grey crowning of the baby, the wispy emergence of the head and the casual plop of the body and legs. This was stomachable. I thought we may as well see it now and get used to it. It's not the done thing for an SP to faint mid-delivery.

But we didn't see much mess. I was expecting buckets of blood and guts all over the sheets, sprayed over doctors and nurses, fountains of muck pouring out of the mother, on to a dripping and screaming neonate. Something like a birth scene from the movie *Alien*. But no, it didn't appear on the video. It was all pretty clean. I was stunned. Friends had said there's blood and mess everywhere. Could they have been exaggerating? Was birth not really as messy as, say, group orthopaedic surgery after a highway disaster? Was that because it was a natural process, with just enough lubricant to let everything slip out with a shove and nothing more? Or was the hospital sanitising the show for us? Had the bloody bits been left on the editing suite floor, not included in the final cut? Surely not. This was supposed to be a class where we learnt what really went on. They wouldn't leave anything out, would they? Would they?

The videos concluded the first day. Most of the group survived it. Mrs Jymfit untangled herself and the Goodtimes continued beaming. Only Gay Fearwarden looked scared, and Adam Happytalk stared solemnly at the floor.

DAILY LIFE IN THE FUTURE

The second day, the following Saturday, began with life post-birth. First up, a break-down of the day. It was put to us like this:

6.00 am	Nappy change
6.30 am	Feed
7.30 am	Play time
8.00 am	Sleep (Baby that is). Shower. Breakfast. Recreational.
11.00 am	Rise. Nappy change.
11.30 am	Feed.
12.30 pm	Play time / Sleep (Baby that is).
3.00 pm	Rise. Nappy change.
3.30 pm	Feed. Play. Bath. Feed. Somewhere eat your own dinner.
8.00 pm	Sleep (Baby that is).
10.30 pm	Rise. Feed.
11.30 pm	Sleep. All of you. While you have the chance.
2.00 am	Rise. Feed.
3.00 am	Sleep.
6.00 am	Repeat from top. There might be an additional night-time feed too.

In all, you get about an hour a day for self. By 'self' was meant extra sleep, exercise, friends, bathing, eating, laundry, or sex. (Note the 'or'). The message was crystal clear: men (as opposed to SPs), don't expect to come home wondering what on earth your wife/partner has been doing all day, wondering how she could be so exhausted when it's only a baby she's looking after. You'll have no time for *anything*. Your life is the baby, and exhaustion. Do not come home expecting sex. Do not come home expecting play. Do not come home expecting a gourmet three-course meal. In fact, do not come home expecting anything except a woman who needs to be helped by you, her SP, for life. There was an air of admonition in the session. Do not pass go, do not collect $200. I sneaked a look around the room. All the men had joined Adam in staring solemnly at the floor, except for Mr Goodtime who beamed perfection at us all.

PRACTICAL TIPS FOR HANDLING KIDS

The next session was a practical one, covering all the little tips for handling kiddies once they're out of the womb. You might think that it all comes naturally, but there are things to be taught, great mysteries of how to look after newborns that need to be mastered. To help us learn these secrets, Dorothy passed around Gidget and some of her stuffed dummy mates to practise on. We had a go at four basic skills:

Nappy-changing: Things were a little more comfortable when we did nappy changing. For this exercise, Gidget the foam foetus, was pulled out of her net uterus, and passed around for a practice run. Nappy-changes first. Disposable ones first, then should they ever be needed, cloth. Dorothy asked 'How many of you have changed a nappy before?' Ruby put up her hand. To her surprise less than half the group had. I wasn't the only one. Dorothy demonstrated. Nappy out ready, bub on its back, up through the legs, stick tab A on tab B and tab C on tab D. 'The trick is to make it firm but comfortable,' advised Dorothy. 'Not too tight, or the baby will be uncomfortable, but not too loose, or it'll fall off.' Ruby grinned at me when Gidget appeared on my lap. She held out a nappy and laid down the challenge, 'Come on first-timer, let's watch you muck it up.'

Much to her surprise I was quite good at it. I wrapped up Gidget firmly and securely. The nappy fitted well and showed no signs of falling off when Ruby shook Gidget. 'You aren't supposed to shake them,' I said.

'I didn't realise you knew so much about caring for babies,' she replied. 'You can change all M's nappies seeing you're so good at it.'

'Well, obviously you're the one who needs the practice,' I smirked, and she rolled her eyes.

Breastfeeding: Breastfeeding comprised a short video followed by practice with the dummies. The important thing to master was the 'latch' which is getting the baby on to the nipple. I'd thought that mother nature took care of that, and the baby just instinctively plugged itself on, but apparently there's a technique to it. A special flick of the wrist, a correct angle to the head. It sounded like a putt from the edge of the green. One by one the women tried it out, attempting to make it look like what they saw on the video. But breastfeeding a cloth dummy is one thing, doing it to your newborn is another. Meanwhile the SPs stood next to their partners and tried to look relevant.

Wrapping: By contrast, we could all get involved in wrapping up a baby. Gidget was handed round with a cotton wrap of about one metre square. There are different techniques, Dorothy advised, but basically it's this: fold in one side or corner, place the bub face up on the wrap, tuck its hands under the fold to stop it scratching itself, then wrap it up. Firm but comfortable. 'They feel secure that way,' she said. I beamed at Ruby as I showed her my effort.

Burping: Babies, it seems are impolite little blighters. They get wind and need to be burped during each feed. Dorothy picked up Gidget and lumped it first on to her shoulder, and then sat it upright on her knee, supporting its limp little neck. Then she whacked it on the back. Not too hard, but harder than I'd anticipated. 'They're pretty resilient little things,' she explained. 'They like it firm but comfortable'.

That was the basic message. Firm but comfortable. I decided that would be the hallmark of my fatherhood. In everything I did I would be firm but comfortable. When M was 30 and I asked her what she thought of my parenting, she would say, 'Dad, if there's one thing which stood out, it's this: you were always firm but comfortable.'

THINGS THAT CAN GO WRONG

After lunch that day we had a discussion about things that can go wrong, a request of the group after a vote. Ruby had put the motion, on the basis that all we'd heard so far was the healthy side of the story, but she wanted some preparation in case something went wrong. There were murmurs of assent and the motion was carried. So, full of hospital cafeteria lunch we re-entered the room to share tales of woe. Dorothy opened the floor.

'Has anyone had any friends with . . .' With what, I wondered. A sad outcome? Problems? Difficulties? '. . . with an unexpected issue?' A what? An unexpected issue? I almost gagged. But the irony of her comment had completely escaped her. Children are issue. So what is an unexpected issue: a boy when you're expecting a girl, or a kid with hooves and horns when you're expecting an angel?

I looked around the room, but no-one else's face registered the irony. Instead, they all waited for someone else to speak. To speak what? Maybe we don't like speaking of – grief – failure – disappointment – unexpected issues. I dived in. Foolishly.

'One friend of ours got to 35 weeks and happened to remark to her obstetrician that she'd not felt the baby kick for a while. The doctor checked it out and told her that she was going in immediately for an emergency caesar and to expect the worst. The foetus had used up all the placenta and had stopped growing, so they couldn't tell what it would be like. It could be deformed, brain-damaged or even worse, stillborn. As it turned out, everything was okay and they have a lovely little son. But it was an 'issue'.'

People listened with concerned expressions that brightened at the happy ending. Obviously this was the type of story to tell – one with a happy ending. 'Very good,' said Dorothy, as if I'd just delivered a testimonial at an AA workshop. 'Anyone else?'

No-one volunteered, so I threw my second bit in. 'Another friend wasn't so lucky. She went full term, and at the last check-up the doctor couldn't detect the heartbeat. She had lupus disease, and didn't know it. The baby had died. What made it doubly hard was they had to induce her and she had to deliver her stillborn baby. It was a boy. They named him, and held him for a while. It was terrible. She's had three kids since then, though.'

This story obviously didn't go down so well. A pall had descended upon the room. Dull faces stared blankly at me. A tear appeared in Mrs Happytalk's eye, and Mrs Fearwarden had gone green. I caught Mrs Jymfit glaring at me from under her left knee. Adam Happytalk stared solemnly at the floor.

'It happens,' said Dorothy resolutely, 'although very rarely. That's why there are midwives and obstetricians.' I was glad the focus had shifted to her. Bravely she continued the group descent into horror.

'So how about after the baby is born? Have we any stories to tell there?' Silence again. I thought I felt some eyes turn in my direction. I picked up the invitation. Foolishly.

'A very close friend of mine – I call him Guru Dave because he's such a fabulous guy – had a bouncing baby boy about five years ago. Four months after he was born, they thought he was blind, because he wasn't tracking properly. He didn't follow things around the room like four-month-old babies should. It turned out he wasn't blind, he was developmentally disabled. They don't know why. They spent six months doing every test possible to find out, but there's no explanation. This was several years ago. He can walk, but he can't talk very much, and he's still in nappies. And he's a really happy kid. The thing is, Guru Dave and his wife are the best people I know. I'm not just saying that. They were great beforehand, but the love and energy they pour into their son is probably more than we'll ever pour into our children combined. As Guru Dave said, 'Our boy will have the best chance in life if we love him as much as we can. So we do it.'

Hey, I tried to end on a positive note, but the group didn't pick it up. I may as well have brought a dead cat into the room. Even the Sunbodies had lost their radiance, and the Goodtimes had stopped holding hands. I think for the first time in 37 weeks the Firetones had a grimace on their faces. Dorothy did her best.

'It can be hard. Childbirth is a very uncertain thing. Despite the best of medical assistance there can be . . .' – be what? I thought, more unexpected issues? 'There can be difficulties.' Ah, difficulties. At least it wasn't an issue.

'Anyone else?' asked Dorothy. Has anyone had friends with a difficulty? No one dared move, let alone talk. All eyes turned to me. Dorothy said, 'You don't have any more stories do you?'

'I don't think you want to hear it,' I replied. Foolish. Foolish. Foolish.

'There's more?' I think even Dorothy was shocked. I repeated. 'I don't think you want to hear any more.' She turned to the group.

'Have we had enough?' Dorothy asked the room.

'No, let's hear it,' said Mrs Happytalk. That kind of made sense in a way. She'd spent every spare moment asking Dorothy every possible question about birth, and now she wanted to hear everything about difficult births. 'I know it's sad, but it's part of the risk,' she added. Encouraged by the only other voice on the floor, Dorothy said, 'Tell us then.'

'A family friend,' I said quietly. 'The baby was fine. But some amniotic fluid somehow entered the mother's bloodstream. She didn't survive. They put pictures of her on the bassinet.'

I was the devil incarnate. I could feel my horns and hooves burning under the heated gaze of the others in the room. This wasn't the kind of stuff you present to a bunch of pregnant hopefuls looking forward to a happy future. But hey, it wasn't just me. The whole group had agreed to talk about these things. Otherwise I wouldn't have said anything. I wondered why we were doing this. To dull ourselves to grief if something happened? But that wouldn't work: experiencing grief doesn't dull its intensity. To reassure us that our futures were safe by listening to the lives of others? But that wouldn't work either: you can't control the future. I think it was the risk factor which Mrs Happytalk had mentioned. There's a deep need to acknowledge that even though we'll do everything to make our children safe, there's so much that can go wrong. I liked Mrs Happytalk for mentioning the risk. I'd felt it from the first month of Ruby's pregnancy. I think we all had. I was also thankful for Mr Faux-Ruby when he lifted the mood a little by saying, 'I'm not going anywhere near your friends.'

GETTING THINGS IN LINE

The final exercise was one aimed at testing our understanding of the mother's expectations of her labour. The SPs were asked to leave, while the women discussed something secret. Then we were called back in and asked to stand in a line along the middle of the room corresponding to a spectrum of where we thought our partners might be in labour – from complete fear of the process and wanting a caesar at one end, to absolute drug-free natural birth at the other. We shuffled around with good humour. Sean Fearwarden got it right as he clung to the window at the caesar end. Ian Sunbody was at the other end under Gloria's gleam of approval. Adam Happytalk found his wife's spot on the floor. Ruby smiled at me when I got hers right. She wanted as natural a birth as possible but was prepared to consider pain relief if needed. So I stood about three-quarters of the way along the spectrum. No-one got it wrong in fact, so we gave ourselves a collective pat on the back.

It was a good ending to the two days. Dorothy wished us all well, and that was it. We had the knowledge. We were trained in birth. We – mother and SP – could go out and deliver a fresh healthy body into the world.

Anytime now. Really, it could happen at any time. I turned to Ruby and asked: 'How was that for you?'

'Good until the very end,' she replied.

'Why was that?'

'As we were leaving I asked Dorothy if she'd had children herself.'

'And?'

'She hadn't. I mean, what good is it telling us this stuff if you haven't been through it yourself? Sure, she's seen lots of births, but she's never had to make the decision from the inside.'

I put my arm around her. 'Then it's just us,' I said. But I felt a bit helpless.

'I'm so glad you're the father,' she said. 'I couldn't do this without you, and I couldn't do it with anyone but you.'

Wow. She earned brownie points for that one.

What's happening to it

Month Eight About 40 cm. Family size pizza.

VITAL STATISTICS

Length:	About 40 centimetres
Weight:	About 2.5 kilos.
Brain:	Getting bigger.
Eyes:	They've usually opened up by now. The little one will be looking around a bit, but I'm not quite sure what at.
Ears / Hearing:	Pretty much fully-formed by now.
Hair:	Lanugo, vernix.
Limbs:	Kicking is quite strong because the foetus is running out of room. It stretches, grabs at things and sucks its thumb.
Skin:	Fat is beginning to develop more now.

What's happening to her

The Frontal Bulge is bulging. All the symptoms and emotions of Month Seven may increase in intensity. She may be stiff and find it difficult to get out of a chair or bed or off the loo. Her feet may be swollen so much that she can't wear shoes. The size of her tummy may mean she has difficulty breathing. There may be pink stretch marks on her belly and abdomen. She may have varicose veins, severe back pain and haemorrhoids. It can be a pretty ugly sight, but don't tell her that.

Add to all that, boredom with her pregnancy, a possible lack of sleep, fatigue, clumsiness and apprehension about the state of the house, the finances, how the birth will go, will the child be safe – she may be becoming a pregnancy monster.

For most, however, it's not so bad, and by the end of Month Eight you know the end is reasonably nigh. Whatever the case, she will still be the most beautiful woman in the world.

What's happening to me

LATE NIGHT RUMINATIONS

One month to go. Four weeks and a bit. (Four weeks and a baby!) Time is measured in weeks now, not months. The countdown is about to begin, if it hasn't already. All the waiting will soon be over. All the wondering, the guessing, will be revealed in four weeks. All the jokes and laughter become serious. Labour will be upon us. The effort and risk of delivery, the ecstasy of birth, and knowledge of our child.

The realisation of how close we were to The Event sent a mixture of wild emotions surging through my brain. Our child. We would have a child. M. A daughter, son, a dependant, someone who would rely on me for everything: food, shelter, emotional support, direction, peace, love. Of course, we had seen her(him) in the ultrasound, and only a few weeks ago. The shape of the head, the arms and legs folded, the curved spine. These were unreal images in fuzzy black and white, as if M was floating, suspended in a snowy night, oblivious to us, to the world, to her(his) orientation and to how she(he) was upended in the womb.

In four weeks time it would be different. We would have, not the weightless image in the ultrasound, but the real thing, a real child. A creature at the start of its life, a living potential. Someone who, even now, I knew would carry my heart into the future. Someone who would be separate from me, but inseparable, reminiscent of me in all that happened, even though I may not always be near, and will, indeed, one day be gone.

An extraordinary sense of joy accompanied these thoughts, along with a deep sense of awe at the responsibility of it all. That I should be responsible for, first, the creation of this little human, and second, his(her) development. It was a scary idea. The birth was scary, because I understood labour to be a risky and difficult business, but life afterwards was even more daunting.

I wondered how Ruby would react to all that was about to happen. What would she need, and how would she cope? What would she have to endure in labour? Would she take to the child, or, as some mothers do, find it difficult to accept motherhood? How would I handle that? Or if she suffered post-natal depression. How would we cope? How would parenthood change our relationship, as it inevitably would, according to every friend with children and every textbook. Despite all we might read, despite all we might talk about or imagine, these were great unknowns. Ideas, hormones, genes, whatever, lie buried deep within us and habituate so much of our daily behaviour that we may not survive the intervention of a child. Who knows how we might react, to each other, to M, or to ourselves. We may not survive, we may be bound closer, we may carry on as before (albeit with a reduced sex life).

Whatever might happen, we had set ourselves on a path we could not resile from. We had made our bed, and we had to lie in it. Or, more accurately we had lain in our bed, and had to live with the consequences, good, bad, hard or easy. How we might fare depended, in part at least, on me. My resources and abilities, my energy, my ability to adapt to new and possibly difficult pressures. I needed resolve, patience and fortitude, and where I could not ground these in my relationship with Ruby or M, I would need to find them in myself alone.

These thoughts filled my head, as I stroked Tiger's velvet ear next to me on the couch in the Grandrubies living room. It was two o'clock in the morning, the dead hours of the night, as the almost inaudible TV tried to distract me with infomercials for ab-flexers, diet powders and anti-ageing creams. Ruby was in our room below, in bed, breathing peacefully. M was probably asleep too. Tiger was almost asleep and seemed untroubled by me twirling her ear as she lay curled up in a ball. Ruby, M, Tiger and me. The birth of a family, I thought, and what will it be like? Tiger growled just a little, and I thought, well at least you sound confident. I looked down and noticed the tell-tale quivering of the eyebrows as she dreamed a doggy dream. She was oblivious to me. Ah well, time I went to bed.

HAVING A COW

The main task for the month (aside from delivering a baby) was to get back into our home. Not an easy prospect when it wasn't built. Most of it was, but it wasn't liveable, especially not for Ruby who was about to bring home a baby. Sure, the basic structural stuff was done – floors, roof, walls – but large parts were still incomplete. Cupboards weren't in, the bathroom wasn't tiled, light fittings had to be installed, painting needed to be done and the floors needed to be polished. Even a non-builder could see there was more than a month's work.

Nevertheless, Ruby said it had to be done within the month. 'I'm not bringing a baby into a half-built house. And I'm not having the painting going on when M gets home . . . heaven knows what the fumes might do. Or nailing or sawing going on when M is trying to sleep.'

The builder – a sunny Italian bloke called Tony whose greatest defence was to agree with everything we said – smiled and reassured us that everything would be done on time. 'We'll get the bathroom floor laid tomorrow and the tiler will come the next day. The bathroom should be finished by Friday.'

'And the cabinets?' asked Ruby.

'The cabinetmaker will come Wednesday when the stairs are finished and the bench top has been installed. You should be able to move in on Saturday.'

Of course, the bathroom wasn't laid tomorrow, the cabinet didn't come on Wednesday and the tiler never came the next day. We weren't able to move in on Saturday.

'Oh yeah, we'll be finished next week,' agreed Tony. Ruby rubbed her Frontal Bulge as M jumped indignantly inside her. 'What about the tiler, where was he?'

'He was stuck on another job,' Tony said, 'but he knows he's due on Monday. We've got him booked in.'

'And the cabinetmaker?'

'Well, he was waiting for the bench top. We have to fit that before the cabinets go in. It won't take more than a day. You can see the cabinets, they're all pre-made.' He waved his hand towards a stack of half-made cabinets covering most of the living room floor. Ruby played the sympathy card, standing in front of Tony in her leggings and polo neck jumper, holding the Bulge in both hands.

'I've got a baby coming in three weeks, maybe two. I won't move in unless everything is finished.' Tears welled in her eyes and she stuck her tummy out further to accentuate her despair.

'Don't worry,' Tony beamed, 'we're working back late to finish it.'

Placated, almost, we went in search of a good pub steak. Dr Q had discovered that Ruby's iron count was very low, and had prescribed an iron supplement, fefol, to boost it. He'd also said that eating red meat wouldn't have that much effect.

'But it won't do any harm, will it?' Ruby asked. All she needed was Dr Q's 'Not at all,' and we were committed to a grilled cow every Saturday for lunch, preferably on a sunny pub balcony somewhere. One week it was on the balcony of the London in Balmain, another on the balcony of the Woolloomooloo Hotel, or on the balcony of the Royal at Paddington where almost eight months ago I'd sat with bachelor Stu and contemplated the future arrival of my child.

Ruby had an insatiable appetite. She ordered the biggest scotch fillet, or New York cut, or oyster blade, or T-bone or entire hind quarter with lashings of hot mustard, a beer and perhaps a side salad, which sent M spinning with the onslaught of a chewed and char-grilled hit of iron. In Ruby's swollen body there was room for either baby or steak, but she seemed to squeeze both in happily, and sit back afterwards in the sun rubbing her belly proudly.

Of course, by the next weekend the bench tops weren't installed, the cabinets not inserted, the bathroom not tiled, the floors not polished, the house nowhere complete.

'Here's a list of things to be done before we move in,' said an angry Ruby with moist eyes.

'Yeah, yeah,' agreed Tony. 'You should be able to move in next weekend. The tiler is coming tomorrow, the bench top will be in on Monday and the cabinets that afternoon.'

'And the painters?' demanded Ruby.

'Wednesday,' said Tony. They had to do the entire house – inside and out. I didn't think so. 'Oh they will,' he said. 'The cabinets will be in place and they can start on the outside any time.'

Off to the London Hotel for half a cow again, Ruby grumbling all the way. 'Am I being unreasonable? Tell me if I'm being unreasonable. Am I?'

'Eat your cow,' I replied.

There were signs of progress, and Tony had been working late, as evident from the visits by local council inspectors during the week responding to complaints from neighbours. I thought I should put up a sign apologising to all the street, explaining that we needed to finish before M arrived. Tony had placated the council officers by agreeing not to work late again and then carried on working.

A team of Korean painters arrived: the Lucky Shine Painting Co. Test swabs of various colours adorned the front wall of the house when we arrived the next weekend. The painting had not actually started yet, but there were signs it might.

The bathroom was tiled and the cabinets were in. Tony showed us the work.

'They're fabulous,' I said. He agreed.

'I don't like them,' said Ruby.

'They're fabulous,' I repeated.

'They're too high.' she said.

'They're what we wanted,' I reminded her.

'I didn't realise they'd be so high,' she said.

'You'll have to live with it,' I said.

'Tell me I like them.'

'You like them.'

'I don't like them.'

'They were on the plans, in the contract, in the specifications. We aren't changing them now. Focus on having M instead.'

She looked down at The Bulge and said, 'What do you think M? Are they too high?'

M didn't care. About the height of the cabinets, or any of the other things that were wrong, whether fixable or not. The colour of the door handles, the way the fridge door opened, the gaps in the paintwork, the chips in the brickwork, the crack in the skylight, whatever. In the scheme of things it didn't matter. The fact there was a list of things to fix was a sign of progress. Cabinets had been installed – now it was time to fix the handles. The doors were in – now it was time to match the keys to locks. And so on. A team of painters crowded the finished areas with drop-sheets, tins of paint and ladders. The builders hung out of the windows repairing locks, windows, balustrades etc. The cabinet-makers were fitting the laundry beneath the stairs, as the electrician installed power points, computer cables and fuse box. The place was a hive of activity aimed as much at finishing the house before M arrived, as showing us that they would finish the house before M arrived.

'Am I being unreasonable?' Ruby asked again, as if on cue, over a slab of char-grilled beef at the Clovelly Hotel. 'Tell me if I'm being unreasonable,' she repeated.

'Eat your cow,' I responded.

'I'll finish yours if you don't want it,' she said.

'I don't know how you squeeze it all in,' I said. 'You have a nine-month-old baby squashed inside, and you're eating four times its size in pure beef.'

'Does it make me look fat?' she asked.

'You're pregnant, not fat. It makes you look pregnant.' She rolled up the thick wool of her polo neck jumper and exposed the stretched shiny ball of her Bulge.

'I'm actually starting to get sick of it,' she confessed. 'I'm starting to want my body back. I don't fit into the same spaces I used to fit into any more.

Whenever I turn around I bump into things. I want my self back.' As if in response to this claim her belly bounced as M thrashed out. 'You see? I didn't do that – it was M.' She stabbed at another piece of beef.

'I thought you were enjoying being pregnant now,' I said.

'I am. Was. Kind of. Am.'

'That definite, huh?'

'Am I being unreasonable?' she asked.

'What about: the cupboards or M?'

'M.'

'Is that why you're grumpy at the house?' I asked.

'No, I'm grumpy at the house because I want it finished before M comes. And I'm grumpy not *at*, but *about* M because I want my body back. I'm huge. Look at me.' I could see. She was nine months pregnant. Women who are nine months pregnant have huge tummies.

'What do you expect? You could drop at any moment.'

'Every time I turn around I bump into things. I have to lean over my tummy all the time – at shops, to wash my hands, whatever. I can hardly sit down or get up. I can hardly tie my shoes. There are loads of things I just can't do. I'm getting sick of it,' she said.

'Does this mean we have to start eating hot curries and castor oil?' I asked.

'What for?'

'To make M come. They say that spicy food helps stimulate the onset of birth. As does running on a trampoline and vigorous sex,' I said knowledgeably. 'They're the four standard ways of bringing on labour.'

'That's all you men think about,' she grumbled.

'What, bringing on labour?'

'No, sex.'

'Hey, I'm just the ideas man,' I said. 'I'm just trying to help you through the process, like any good Support Person.'

'Well sex is the last thing on my mind,' she warned me.

This encounter drove home to us the imminence of The Day. It could be now. It could be tomorrow. Or next week. It could be delayed. We just didn't know. As a precaution Ruby packed her hospital bags. She read out to me a list of goodies some of the books suggested we might take : CDs, candles, incense and aromatherapy stuff. Please, I thought. We're having a baby, not attending a bloody folk festival. Ruby went for the basics: a change of clothes, toiletries and hair-dryer. Bulky pads for discharges. A little bag of readiness stood by our bedroom door, reminding us of the closeness of The Day.

MOVING IN AND TRADITIONAL WAYS
NUMBERS 1, 2 AND 3

By a miracle of construction and human effort, the house was sufficiently finished by the weekend for us to consider the possibility of planning to move in
during the week. Sure, the floors needed a couple of days to dry, the paint
smell needed a couple of days to disperse, and the cabinets needed a couple
of days to shrink, but hey, that was only a couple of days and then we would
be in. Hooray! I saw a smile flash across Ruby's pink face.

'We have a home,' she said, and leaned over the gulf of her Bulge to hug
me. 'You see?' she said. 'I can hardly reach you.' I had to admit, she was
getting big.

'How about we celebrate by eating a water buffalo this weekend?' I
suggested.

'I thought I might try a curry today,' she replied. Hello hello, I thought,
now we have the house, she's ready to fill it with a baby. That's Ruby, always
wanting to organise the timetable. Sorry, honey, it doesn't necessarily work
that way. M will come, timetable or not.

Although, I had to admit, Ruby may have actually done it. Only four or five
days away from the official due date, we finally got the nod to move in. Tony
had come through. Not that the house was actually finished. The painters
were still outside, builders were fixing last-minute items, and the electrician
was still trying to get all of the lights working. But it was enough for us to
leave our underground rooms beneath the Grandrubies and head home.

I looked back on the last few months as I bounced along in the front seat
of the removalist van. A new house, a new car, a new carport, a new cot, a new
pram, a new mountain of new nappies, jumpsuits, singlets and other baby
paraphernalia. And a new baby on the way. A new life in fact. The move was
almost a rite of passage, an induction into my new status as a mortgage rich,
cash poor, child rich, sex poor, neo-parent.

I say almost a rite of passage because the move did not have the dignity of
a real transitional ceremony. It was more like a battlefield. It was a rainy
Wednesday. Armies of grandparents and removalists and painters and
builders clambered between boxes and paint tins and furniture swathed in
plastic. Chairs, lamps, books, cases, linen and dust bins were passed beneath
ladders, around the cement mixer and into the house, over the sticky plastic
sheet the removalists had laid down to protect the polished floors from
muddy feet. Everything was higgledy-piggledy. Picture frames were in the
kitchen, stacked chairs were in the bedroom, the TV was in the bathroom,

bed linen and books in the stereo cabinet, dumped by many helping hands anxious to avoid the downpour.

Then into this bedlam strode The Bulge, with Ruby close behind. She established her largeness in the one armchair that had actually made it into the living room, and from there directed the flow of traffic like a fat general commanding troops on the field.

'That chair goes there. The light goes in the corner. The saucepans in that cupboard. The trampoline upstairs.'

'The what?' I asked.

'I borrowed it from a friend who isn't using it,' she replied, ignoring my sarcasm.

'No-one ever does,' I responded and then heard my mother ask, 'Does the castor oil go in the pantry here?' Ruby grinned at me guiltily. 'Just in case,' she protested. I thought of our first meeting with Dr Q all those months ago, and realised not even professional medicine could defeat old wives' tales. There was only the fourth birth stimulant to get a mention now – sex. Between castor oil, jungle curry and trampolines, sex was a better option, even if it was for the purposes of inducing labour. I made a mental note not to act surprised when she wanted sex next time, but to ensure the hospital bags were packed in case it proved effective. And, of course, to look like I'm eager for the opportunity.

Miraculously, the chaos in the house finally settled itself into some sort of order, despite the constant patter of the rain and the dark skies. As the grey day lengthened, the builders disappeared one by one, taking ladders and tool boxes with them. The painters packed up their tins and drop-sheets and loaded them into their vans. The removalists backed their truck out of the driveway. Both sets of grandparents took their leave after a cup of tea, made from a kettle which had found its way into the kitchen. It replaced the picture frames which had moved into various rooms ready for hanging. The TV had relocated from the bathroom into the living room. The chairs had moved into the living room, to make space for the bed linen which had moved from the stereo cabinet to make space for the stereo. Everything was finding its place: books on shelves, crockery in cupboards, the car in the carport, Ruby in a chair and M inside Ruby.

I surveyed the scene. 'Just one last thing to do,' I said. 'I'll pull up the plastic the removalists put down to protect the floors.' I lifted up one end and tugged. It was stuck. I pulled harder, and it resisted. So I pulled more and it lifted reluctantly, bringing large gobs of floor varnish with it. As I pulled up more of the plastic, more varnish bubbles came with it, leaving a moon-cratered runway down the main living room and hallway to the front door. The floor was ruined. I don't remember which expletive I used first, but I think I ran through the list.

Ruby staggered to her feet and stared at it, then muttered, 'Just something else to contend with.' She sat down again. 'This place is a mess,' she said, sweeping her hand around the room.

'Of course it is,' I replied, 'We've just moved in.' I suddenly realised that she was about to explode. What I'd thought was just logistical efficiency on her part had in fact been a ticking time bomb. Don't tell me the crankies had returned to spoil the last few days of pregnant bliss, I thought. I steeled myself with as much compassion and elephant hide as I could muster in the micro-second before she exploded.

'I'm exhausted. I'm about to have a baby. I've got a huge body. Look at me. This place just isn't anywhere near ready for M to arrive and now the floor is ruined. What are we going to do?' I wondered what the best response was, and probably wondered a bit too long, because she asked, 'Well?' So I replied, 'We have a new house, a new car, a new cot, a new pram, a new baby on the way and a new life about to begin. What we're going to do is enjoy it, floor or no floor. It's only a hiccup in the scheme of things. M won't care if the floor is cratered. What she will care for is the wonderful mother that you're going to be.' Ruby wrapped her arms clumsily around my hips and hugged me from her sitting position, her head resting awkwardly on the front of my pants. She said, 'I just want everything to be all right. I'm scared of the

Then into this bedlam strode The Bulge, with Ruby close behind. She established her largeness in the one armchair that had actually made it into the living room, and from there directed the flow of traffic like a fat general commanding troops on the field.

labour, partly because of what I will be going through, but mainly for M. I don't want anything to happen to her.' I stroked her hair.

'It's going to be fine. You're going to be fine. M's going to be fine.' I reassured her.

'How do you know?' she asked.

'Easy. I speak from complete ignorance.' She snorted. I went on, 'But I do know a few things. You're my wife. You're healthy, fit and very focussed. I have the utmost confidence in you. And M is your child so she'll be just the same. In fact, she is probably cleaning out the womb now so it's ready for the next occupant.' Ruby hugged me closer. 'And another thing,' I added, 'Talking to my groin won't get you anywhere.' There was a loaded pause and I thought I'd blown it, but she said, 'Why not? It got me into this predicament. Give me a hand up. I'm going to bed.'

'I've got to make it first,' I said.

THE GRUMPIES RETURN

The next few days were a bumpy ride. Ruby was constantly grumpy, tired, sick of her Bulge or withdrawn. She sat silently, sometimes watching the sky, as if internally psyching herself for the impending labour. Other times she banged around the house, trying to impose some order on the boxes of stuff that had been dumped in the various rooms and had not yet been emptied. She angrily conceded that we had no photographic record of her pregnancy, so I took a few shots of her leaning on the fireplace, glaring at the camera as the Great Pink Bulge swelled over the red tracksuit pants.

MOVING OUT AND TRADITIONAL WAY NUMBER 4

The down-side was that the entire floor needed to be resealed. So we had to move out again. The removalists put us up in a nearby serviced apartment, advising that the floor would need about four to five days to settle. We packed our bags, including the hospital bags and left as the removalists shipped our stuff out again.

The serviced apartment was as I imagined serviced apartments would be (not having had the luxury of staying in one before). A bed, a bathroom with a faulty shower hose, a table with cane chairs and stained beige couches. It was home enough for this short period. On the first night Ruby called to me from the bedroom as I tried to fix a crackle on the TV.

'I'm sick of this!' shouted the bedroom.

'What?'

Bzz, fzz, said the TV.

'I said I'm sick of this,' the bedroom repeated.

'Okay, I hear you.'

Bzz, fzz, said the TV again.

'Did you hear me?' yelled the bedroom.

'I said I heard. What are you sick of?' I called back, trying to squeeze my big fingers around impossibly small nobs on the TV. They crackled mockingly at me. Bzz, fzz.

'Being pregnant,' bellowed the bedroom.

'Well take some castor oil if you want to bring it on,' I shouted back.

Bzz, fzz, said the TV.

'It's in the cupboard at home.' The tone of her voice made me realise she was in danger of revoking permission for me to meet Guru Dave and Single Stu for a drink that evening. I began to wonder what tack I should take to appease her.

'And the trampoline?' I called.

'At home.'

'I could order you a curry,' I suggested.

'I'm not hungry.'

Bzz fzz, said the TV. I had my hand up its rear and was trying to fiddle with the aerial plug.

'I'm fed up with this!' An unsettling note of frustration and impatience had entered her voice. I felt the hairs on my neck rise.

'I'm sorry, there's not much I can do,' I said. Bzz, fzz, said the TV. I thumped it and buried my head in the black hole of the cupboard to see if I could figure out the problem. Suddenly, Ruby was on top of me. I froze, suddenly aware of her intent.

'Yes there is,' she said, in a low threatening tone. 'You can have sex with me.' Slowly, I extracted my head from the cupboard and looked up at her. She was stark naked. From below, in my crouching position, the Bulge was enormous. She stuck out like a beer barrel, with two dangling red tits on either side like warning bells. Her hair was wild, her eyes were bloodshot and there was a look of fierce determination on her face. I felt my heart stop. Bzz, said the TV, no fzz.

'Have sex with me,' said Ruby, with a look that added 'or die'. I motioned dissent. 'Have sex with me,' she insisted. I struggled to get up, but she thrust her Bulge towards me.

'Have sex with me!' Her tone was desperate.

'Sweetheart –' I began.

'Have! Sex! With! Me!' she shouted.

It was the last thing I wanted to do. This was no seduction. This was a woman desperate to use any means to rid herself of an alien inside her, whether the person she used (me) survived or not. It was not a turn-on. My mind flitted to the pub, where images of dark wood, golden beer and low lights beckoned.

'Have sex with me,' she said again. I tried to think how best to escape. I looked over to the front door. It was three metres away, on the other side of Ruby. My legs wanted to run for it. My mind feared she would tackle me. My conscience thought I should be more diplomatic. I figured I would try negotiating first, and if that failed, make a run for it. I took her in my arms, tried my best to exude comfort and not lust.

'Sweetheart, having sex with you isn't going to bring on labour any more than hot curries, trampolines or castor oil.'

'How do you know?'

'You aren't officially due for another two days. There's no reason for M to come now –'

'Yes there is . . . me!'

'And besides, the first is often late. The body itself will dictate when M comes, and you have a particularly healthy and attractive body.'

'Attractive?'

'Yes.'

'Even though it's this big?'

'Yes.' I thought I was on a winner now.

'Then why won't you have sex with me?' No winner here I thought as she continued, 'I thought you'd grab the chance of a poke on offer.'

I replied, 'Not with an angry pregnant woman who just wants to do it to bring on labour. Grant me some dignity.' Ruby took a step back and laughed a little. I felt a mixture of relief and suspicion.

'You're scared, aren't you? Scared you might just be used for a step in child birth.'

'No, it's not that –' I lied.

'I've got news for you, bucko. I've been used for the last nine months. M doesn't care about me. I'm just the vehicle she uses to get born. Well I want out, and if you have to get used to get me out, that's poetic justice. Get your clothes off.'

So much for diplomacy. My keys were on the cane table. My wallet was on the coffee table. The door was behind Ruby. She would be slow, with all the added weight of the Bulge. If I rushed I could just make it.

'Okay,' I said. 'There's just one thing I have to do.' I sidled over to the dining table and grabbed my keys.

'What?' she asked. I dashed around her to my wallet and leapt to the door.

'Boast about it beforehand to Stu and the Guru. I'm off to the pub.' And with that I sprang through the door, slamming it behind me on a stream of expletives.

As I drove to the hotel, I judged that enough time had passed for her distemper to subside and rang her on my mobile. She was asleep.

'Wazzup?' she mumbled.

'I've got the mobile on in case something does happen.'

'Mmm.'

'You will ring me, won't you?'

'Grzzz, blmmmp.' Was I talking to Ruby or the TV?

TAKING THE CALL

The pub was as pubs are. Drinks were drunk, stories told, cigarettes smoked below the silent TV footage of horses racing somewhere in the world. A million miles from childbirth, or fears of childbirth, or attempted childbirth. For many people, this is where it all begins. Boy at pub meets girl at pub, buys her a drink, they talk and laugh and think . . . maybe someday . . . The mobile rang. The screen said it was Ruby. It seemed like the whole pub fell silent as I answered.

'It's me. I've had some pains, and I went to the toilet and I think I've had the show. There was a browny tinge. I don't know, so I rang the hospital and they said to come in and have a look, so I thought I'd ring you to see what you're doing.'

To see what I'm doing. What does she think I might be doing? Hanging around here while she nicks out to have my child? As if I have some casual interest in my child being born, and she thought she should mention it in passing. I mean, really, to see what I'm doing. This could be it. This could be the birth of my son/daughter, and she's asking me what I'm doing?

'I'm coming to get you,' I shouted as the noise of the pub began to rise again. 'Hold on, and don't give birth until I get there!'

Single Stu shouted to the crowd, 'Hey everybody, this guy's wife is about to have a baby. Now!' A group nearby turned in our direction. 'Yeah, him,' said Stu. 'He's off to have a sprog, right this moment!'

'Then it must be your shout,' someone said. But I was leaving, my mind on Ruby and M.

Back at the apartment, Ruby was sitting on the dining room chair in her pregnancy uniform. She had the bags beside the door. I hugged her and said, 'Let's go.' We drove to the hospital at lightning speed. It was about 10.30 pm.

We knew where to go. On the sixth floor we were directed through the heavy swing doors of the maternity unit into a labour room. A lady entered

174 DIARY OF A PREGNANT DAD

the room wearing a badge with the name 'Margaret'.

'Are you a midwife?' I asked.

'Yes,' she replied, and directed Ruby to change out of her leggings and jumper into a backless hospital gown. She attached a foetal heart monitor and took Ruby's pulse. The familiar rowing noise of M's heartbeat pulsed from the machine. Ruby explained her symptoms.

'Let's see how dilated you are then,' replied Margaret, and she pulled a rubber glove out of the box beside the bed. She lubricated it with a white cream, and, gently holding Ruby's right knee in her left hand, deftly inserted her right hand into Ruby's vagina. There was no ceremony here, just procedure. No acknowledgment of Ruby's privacy, or embarrassment. Just procedure. Get used to it, I thought, there's worse to come. Margaret extracted her hand and artfully removed the glove.

'You aren't dilated yet,' she announced as she washed her hands.

'But is this the beginning of labour?' I asked.

'Could be,' she replied. 'It may be just an initial twinge, it may be the start of full labour.'

'So, what does that mean – do we go home and wait, or stay here?'

'Stay here for the moment,' Margaret replied. 'We'll check again in a little while, to see if anything's happening, but it's more than likely you'll stay here.' She left.

I looked at Ruby and squeezed her hand. This was it. I felt strangely disappointed. I don't know why. Maybe I'd anticipated unconsciously that I would be more prepared than I was. I'd been at work all day, and at a sweaty pub all night. I needed a shower and a rest. I thought of the long dark night ahead, with the cold grime of 24 hours on the job, tired and trying to do my best for Ruby. Damn. Oh well. If it had to be, it had to be. Childbirth comes like a thief in the night. Ironic really. You've been expecting for nine months, and it happens so unexpectedly.

Ruby was nervous, and we held each other as close as pregnant bellies and hospital beds allow. I suppressed my desire to join her on the narrow sheets and go to sleep. It wouldn't be right for the Support Person to steal a kip in the middle of the action. I said to Ruby, 'Are you all right?' She smiled wanly, and nodded. I wanted to tell her I loved her. I wanted to tell her I was proud of her. I wanted to tell her it was going to be all right. I wanted to tell her I would help her and not fall asleep, that she would be okay, that our life was about to change, that my heart was full of admiration and fear for her, as well as courage, preparedness, determination, apprehension and longing. I also wanted to grab a sleep. But it was all too much to fit into a sentence, so I just told her the first thing, and we submitted ourselves to hospital time. Hum de hum.

The minutes clicked by. I think I dozed off. Damn. We chatted for a bit. Superficial stuff: work, Tiger, the weather. I might have dozed again. So might Ruby. The hours turned slowly. If this was childbirth, it was a dull start.

At about 1.00 am Margaret reappeared, her cheery smile cutting through the torpor of the delivery suite. I wondered how many babies she'd delivered in the last few hours. In her life.

'Do you have kids?' I asked.

'I have grandkids,' she replied, slapping on a glove and a fistful of lubricant. 'Let's see what's happening.' With that she launched an inquisitive finger into Ruby's innards and paused, looking at nothing and nobody in particular as she assessed the possibility of dilation. When she pulled out she announced:

'No, nothing happening yet. What you felt was probably just the beginnings of it all – early signs that labour is about to begin.'

'So what does that tell us?' I asked.

'Not much,' she replied. 'It could mean you'll start labour tomorrow. It could settle down and wait for a few days. There's no use staying here. Go home, get a good night's sleep and see what happens in the morning.'

So M, you're not coming out tonight. I was relieved. Bed beckoned. I might get some preparation after all. I held Ruby close as we walked up the stairs to the apartment, leaving her bags in the car just in case.

'You okay?' I asked, and she nuzzled my neck. I felt the force of her soul lean into me, deep, sombre and mysteriously elated as she murmured, 'Put me to bed.'

What's happening to it

Month Nine About 45 cm. Frying pan.

VITAL STATISTICS

Length: About 45 centimetres.

Weight: About 3.5 kilos.

Brain, Eyes, Ears, Limbs, Skin, Hair, everything: All ready to go.

In most cases the baby's head-down, and towards the end of the month may even engage, that is, place its head at the top of the cervix.

A bum-first or leg-first baby is called *breech position*. Occasionally, the baby lies across the womb in a transverse position. Either of these could well result in the need for a caesar.

It's ready to come out.

What's happening to her

More of Month Eight, if she's not going into labour already.

The day

What happened

Woken from slumber I felt Ruby's lips brush my cheek with a kiss. 'We're going to have a baby!' I stirred. Darkness seeped from my brain like bath-water down a plug hole. 'Mmm – grr – hmm. What?' Light flitted into my head like a moth. 'The contractions have started,' said Ruby. My eyes opened and I could see her hair over her face as she knelt on the bed beside me. I still didn't quite get it. 'What time is it?'

'Six o'clock. But I've been awake since five.' I closed my eyes as drowsiness weighed down my brain. I let Ruby continue while I eased into consciousness. 'The contractions have started. This time with pain. It's not too bad, like a period cramp, but more regular.' So do we have to go to hospital straightaway? I thought. I hoped not. That would mean forcing myself awake and rushing around. Did I have time for a shower and a shave? I didn't like the idea of spending the day in a hot delivery suite still mired in sleep. Not that I should complain. Are the bags packed? Yes, I remembered, they were.

Mercifully, Ruby said, 'You don't need to get up straightaway. I'll make some tea,' and with a bounce of the mattress she was gone. She seemed remarkably buoyant for someone about to embark on one of life's most painful journeys.

Not long after, she reappeared with two strong cups of tea and sat on the bed. 'Oi, Mr Sleepy, wake up.' I forced myself up on one elbow and sipped, looking at Ruby's smiling face. 'We're going to have a baby,' she said. And we looked at each other, eye to eye, and felt the depth of what was about to happen engulf our hearts. 'I'd better get ready,' I said, and swung my feet over the side of the bed.

'No hurry,' she replied. 'It isn't too bad. I rang the hospital and they said there was no need to go in straightaway. I wouldn't want to anyway. It'd be too boring. I'll make some toast instead.' Great service, I thought, as I showered. I must get her pregnant again. But she'd changed her mind about breakfast. 'Will you take me down to the beach? We can walk around until it's time to go to the hospital. The fresh air will do me good. We can eat something at a café.'

We drove down to Bronte beach. It was a clear blue winter's day. The sky was cloudless, the sea calm and green, the beach awash with gentle even waves. We strolled along the concrete beach-front, arm in arm. There were very few people there, and no-one seemed to notice when Ruby halted mid-step, leaned forward and groaned slightly. We walked on towards Tamarama, Ruby pausing every now and then to allow contractions to pass. I didn't want to stray too far from the car in case things became urgent, but she was adamant that walking would be more comfortable. At her insistence I telephoned my parents to inform them that things had begun. Fighting over the phone, they were horrified to learn that we were not at the hospital.

'You get her over there right away,' my father said.

'Ooh, I'd be at the hospital if I were you,' my mother interrupted.

'Anything could happen, anytime,' shouted Dad from behind her.

'I don't want my grandchild born in the car,' said Mum over the top of him.

'Think of the upholstery,' shouted Dad. But Ruby was insistent, and found her supporter when she called her mother.

'Oh no, you don't want to go to hospital just yet. It's such a lovely day. You'll have plenty of time in the labour ward.' That was double-edged. So we wandered up to the Tamarama Headland, silently anticipating the day ahead. We walked hand in hand, and I stroked her back when she leaned over a park bench for a contraction. After one contraction, she straightened up and said, 'Did you see that?' I hadn't. 'A whale. There's a whale out there.' A whale? Are we whale-watching while giving birth? Is this an episode from the *New Age Guide to Birthing*? Just a tick and I'll get a shaman to chant something and wave a few herbs about. Maybe it would be a pain-free labour after all. And maybe whales could fly, too. I scanned the flat sea in hope of sighting the omen of good fortune, but my eyes drifted back to Ruby and my thoughts to M.

'There,' said Ruby, 'you can see its tail.' But I'd missed it, looking at her instead. 'Come on,' she said, 'it's heading south. Let's hurry back to Bronte so we can see it going.' She took a dozen eager steps before doubling over again. 'That was a mistake,' she said as she straightened up, pink-faced. 'Let's go and get some breakfast. I feel like a couple of poached eggs.' Water, whales, eggs – was everything potent with birth meanings or was it just me?

After breakfast we returned to the apartment. I read. She dozed, and rolled around in bed. About 1.00 pm she emerged looking calm and rested. 'They've almost stopped,' she said, 'there's almost no pain. I don't think anything's going to happen.' We wondered what to do. Ruby had had the show but her waters hadn't broken and the contractions had – well – contracted.

'Maybe you should go into work,' she said, 'it doesn't look like anything's going to happen here for a while. I'll have plenty of time to ring you.'

I hesitated. What if it came on suddenly? 'I'll hang around for a bit, just in case. I'll duck up the street and buy us some lunch.'

I didn't anticipate much would happen in twenty minutes, but when I returned Ruby was on all fours on the couch. She looked up at me with a mixture of fear and resolve. 'They've come back,' she said, and bowed her head as a wave of pain flooded through her. 'And this time they mean business. I think this is it. Eat your sandwich and then take me to hospital.' What did she mean eat my sandwich? She was starting labour. Was I going to sit there and eat a meal while she groaned on the floor? 'I'm not thinking of you. I'm thinking of me. I don't want you distracted by hunger because you missed out on lunch and you can't help me push.' I protested. 'Eat!' she snapped.

I ate quickly as I helped her down the stairs, bits of beetroot and tomato spraying on to the carpet. Ruby stopped halfway down the stairwell and groaned. The trip was only five minutes. In the hospital lift, the bell rang, and the number lit up for Level 6. This is it, I thought, the place we'd visited and the event we'd imagined was about to happen.

But the door didn't open.

The door didn't open! Ruby bent over and groaned. I banged the button. No response. My baby is going to be born in the lift! So much for the bloody whales! Ruby groaned again. How far apart were the contractions? I looked at the other occupants. An elderly woman – in her seventies I'd say – poised and neatly dressed. She would've had kids, and grandchildren no doubt. She'd know what to do. A young mother with a toddler in a stroller. She'd know what to do. Might get distracted by the kid though, his innocent eyes gazing up at me, ignorant of the turmoil that was about to descend upon us. Another woman in a checked jumper and leggings, looking like a midwife might look if a desperate father-to-be desperately wanted someone to look like a midwife. Ruby groaned again. I looked at the floor of the lift. Not much room – we'd have to fold up the stroller. That knocks the mother out. She'd have to look after junior in the corner. The old lady wouldn't take up too much room. I had visions of the obstetrician being winched through the lift ceiling. I looked up for the escape hatch. This was not the movies. I banged the buttons again. Ruby bent over with a dull groan. I stared at Mrs Checktop for sympathy. 'I'm a midwife,' she said, 'but the lift should open.' She must be a midwife, talking positive like that. I banged the buttons again. The lift shuddered. Ruby moaned. Come on you bastard. Ruby groaned again, and squeezed my hand. The number 6 disappeared from above the door. I heard a bell ring. And miraculously the doors opened. Phew!

I led Ruby and the others through the crowd waiting for the lift, like Moses parting the Red Sea. On to the promised land, or at least the delivery suite. It was 1.30 pm.

Our midwife, an Englishwoman called Jacqueline, put Ruby in a hospital cloak and sat her on the bed. I spread our belongings about. Jacqueline took down particulars like hospitals always do. Age, weight, allergies, likes, dislikes, favourite colour etc. She checked M's heartbeat with the foetal heart monitor. She checked Ruby's blood pressure. All symptoms normal. Contractions about five minutes apart. Jacqueline left us to it, off to attend to other mothers in labour. There were six suites. Six women in labour at that very moment. I listened for screams through the wall. I heard nothing.

Ruby groaned and bent forward. I held her hand. How bad would contractions get? I wondered. Ruby seemed to be holding up. What should I be doing? I cast my mind back to Baby School. Wait, assist, comfort, attend. My eyes drifted around the room. On the wall behind the bed, there were splatters of . . . dried blood. How did they get behind the bed? I knew there would be lots of blood, but behind the bed? They didn't tell us this in Baby School. What on earth had gone on in here? And more importantly, would it happen to us? Poor Ruby. The staff were, of course, apologetic when I asked one of them to clean it off.

Jacqueline came in again. Covering a rubber-clad finger in lubricant, she prepared to test how far Ruby had dilated. I was reminded of how medical the process is: one gloved hand on a knee, the other gloved and creamed and stuffed into her vagina. Jacqueline felt for the cervical gap. Ruby looked down dubiously. She was more used to it than I. Jacqueline withdrew a messy finger and announced that Ruby was one centimetre dilated. Only a centimetre. Poor Ruby. Another nine to go. She looked disheartened. The contractions had been bearable, but had got her only ten percent of the way there. Her eyes said it all. What more do I need to go through to get my ten centimetres? I thought of the blood on the wall.

By now the contractions had intensified a little. Ruby squatted down beside the bed, or leaned against the bed, swaying her hips, or kneeled on the bed, breathing through the pain. Her body was becoming less hers. As the pain increased, the physical processes began taking over, entirely independent of her.

By 3.00 pm the contractions had increased to one every four minutes. Good, healthy, gutsy contractions. Painful, uncontrollable, intestinal contractions.

Poor Ruby. She danced a slow dance about the room, swaying with the pain, groaning every four minutes. I massaged her back, and gave her a little water, tried to encourage her as much as possible. But it was her pain, and I've never been through anything like it. The best I could do was assist, and fulfil her requests. She kept it up for another hour.

Jacqueline suggested that a hot bath might help ease the pain, so I ran the bath, deep and warm. Between contractions Ruby stripped off and stepped in. Every four minutes she raised herself on to her knees as the contractions swelled, groaning as they passed. I massaged her lower back as she rocked, head bent, focussing on the end of contractions, as the bath waters washed about her.

But the bath worked too well. By about 4.30 pm., the contractions had diminished. They were coming every ten minutes, and with far less intensity, very similar to this morning. It seemed the hot water had relaxed Ruby and slowed the process. What to do?

We discussed it with Jacqueline, using hospital-speak for a solution. We (they) could induce Ruby with an injection of syntocinon. Her waters hadn't broken yet. We (they) could break her waters, and see what happened. She (not they) could go home. No, she didn't want that, but what exactly did she want?

It was not so much a decision to be made but a resolve to be harnessed. We (she) had a baby inside, which was going to come out somehow, sometime. 'It may as well be now,' said Ruby, and I looked at her with admiration. Jacqueline rang Dr Q, who luckily was in the hospital. He arrived not long after looking calm and organised as always. He put on the rubber gloves and explored inside Ruby. 'The good news,' he said, 'is that you're three centimetres dilated.' Yay! The first phase of labour over. Only two to go. Boo! Only three centimetres. Seven more to go. He gave us the options again: go home, induce and/or break waters. Baby's head, he suggested, was probably being cushioned behind the amniotic sac, so progress had slowed. Put bluntly, there wasn't enough violence to cause the contractions to continue. The baby's head is used as a battering ram to force the cervix open, crushed into the narrow opening by the severe contractions of the uterus.

Ruby looked at me. She didn't want to go home, having come so far. The thought of more days at three centimetres did not appeal. She didn't really want inducement. I suggested she opt for breaking her waters, and if that didn't work she could consider inducing. Jacqueline handed Dr Q a plastic implement much like a crochet needle: long and thin with a little hook at the end. He lubricated it and inserted it into Ruby's vagina, and when he pulled back a flow of greenie-brown liquid flowed from her, like a dirty creek. This is something I'd never seen before – stuff flowing from Ruby's vagina. Sure, I knew woman bleed, but I'd never seen it actually *happen*. But here was liquid, like a muddy creek water, flowing out of her. Uugh.

'That's meconium,' said Dr Q. Obviously he'd seen it before. 'Baby has done a poo inside the sack. It's nothing to worry about, but we'll have to continue monitoring to make sure there's no problem later on.' I hated this hospital-speak, this measured assessment of risk. A potential problem, not to worry about, need to keep an eye on it. It was a curious balance.

So we had to continue. (Like we had a choice). The door hadn't even closed behind him when the contractions kicked back in with a vengeance. This was real pain now. Every two minutes a pounding contraction would crunch Ruby into a ball, and spit pain across her face. She beat the bed with her foot, and groaned and yelled. It was sickening seeing her suffer like this. There would be a couple of minutes rest, during which she would breathe heavily and wait in apprehension for the next onslaught. When it came, it hit her harder. She buckled over, rolling on the bed, banging her feet, eyes closed, mouth set, hanging on for grim life. I felt my massages were feeble in light of her pain, but she said she relished them. 'Just knowing you care is helpful,' she said, and gritted her teeth for the next internal wave. How can a person's body do this to itself? And what of the baby? Was it time for drugs?

'You could have an epidural,' said Jacqueline.

'I don't want to yet,' Ruby replied breathlessly.

'There are no prizes for bravery,' said Jacqueline.

'How did our parents go through this?' asked Ruby.

'How about a bath?' suggested the midwife.

'No, I don't want to slow it down again,' said Ruby, on all fours, with her head at the base of the bed. Now I saw how blood might have got on to the bed-head. 'I've gone this fa-aaarrrgggh!' as another intestinal blow ground her into the sheets, groaning out the pain. I was worried she'd exhaust herself.

'What else is there?' she asked.

'There's pethidine,' replied Jacqueline.

'Doesn't that make you throw up, or go giddy?' Ruby asked.

'It can.'

'I want to remain conscious as much as possible.'

'There's gas. It's not as effective as pethidine, but some women find it helps.'

'Doesn't it taste horrible though?'

'Some say so. Others are fine. It's got better over the years,' said Jacqueline. Ruby was about to say something when a contraction hit her gut again and she doubled over in agony. Towards the end she looked up at me and yelled, 'This is it! We're only having one!' And her eyes drilled mine. I held her hand. When the contraction finished Jacqueline and I withdrew the concertinaed blue pipe from the gas machine on the wall and passed it to Ruby.

'Suck in when the pain is just about to start and keep on sucking as it goes. Make the ball rattle so you know you're getting gas. Go!' Ruby sucked as a contraction sent her scrambling up the wall behind the bed. Muffled cries escaped from her mouth between throaty gasps of gas. The ball rattled, her foot thumped the bed, the bed shook and as the contraction passed she relaxed the gas and moaned. She collapsed on the bed like a wounded warrior, clinging to the metal bars of the bed-head. How long could she keep this up for? Another contraction hit. She sucked gas, the ball rattled, the bed rattled, she yelled and beat the bed with a flailing foot. And again, and again. An incessant repetitive onslaught of pain deep within her, beating our baby's head against the cervix. Using brute violence to force the skull of our future child as a lever to open the cervix. Our little M, a ram-rod of intense agony. Poor M. Poor Ruby.

By 5.00 pm the contractions had increased to every second minute. I hadn't thought they could get much worse, but I was wrong. Only a minute between left Ruby without any real rest. The contraction hit, she groaned and shook, sucked gas and beat her curled toes on the bed. It paused and she knelt where she was, catching a few awkward breaths before the contractions came round again. Her body was expelling this thing, come what may, and come what injury it might cause. The contraction hit again, and ravaged her shaking, gasping body. It went, and her eyes were vacant, her face drawn. It returned. Ruby's cheek pressed against the bed-head as the force thrashed her about and about, sucking on the gas, the ball rattling. It went and came again, and rattled her brittle frame mercilessly, like some great malevolent force with its prey. 'Thus you are born of pain,' it said, 'and pain shall be your beginning.'

In the brief minute's respite, Jacqueline suggested an epidural. 'You can't feel anything. Your whole lower half is completely numb. Why don't I call the anaesthetist so you can discuss it with him?' Ruby nodded numbly as a contraction attacked her again and the midwife was gone.

Twenty-five minutes – and about ten shattering contractions later – the anaesthetist entered the room, all brisk and official behind his large spectacles. The man lacked any bedside manner whatsoever.

'So you want an epidural,' he announced.

'I haven't decided yet,' cried Ruby feebly as the contraction receded.

'I thought you wanted it. I was called in,' said the red beard below the spectacles.

'I want to discuss how it works. What effect it might have on the birth,' said Ruby. 'It stops the pain,' he said. Another contraction swept through Ruby, throwing her against the bed-head as she desperately sucked in the gas. 'Do you want the epidural?' he asked.

'Not yet,' said Ruby. 'Let me discuss it with my husband.' The anaesthetist turned and walked out, a faint air of wounded dignity wafting after him.

'He was horrible,' said Ruby, 'he didn't understand what I wanted.' Jacqueline came in, a much more welcome participant. 'We'll need to decide soon, otherwise you may have a considerable delay. The anaesthetist has another woman in suite three close to giving birth and a caesar about to start.' Ruby looked at me.

'What do you think?' she asked, and then bent over as a contraction savaged her. I held her hand as she thrashed about on the bed, watching her toes curl in pain, and her feet bang the sheets in a frail attempt to dissipate the agony. She gasped, she yelled, she droned and the contraction dragged her down the bed. Her eyes seemed to be asking me to make the decision for her, or at least validate her decision.

'You don't have to go through this. Sick people have pain relief for far less than this. You aren't sick. But you're in a lot of pain. There's no reason why you shouldn't take some relief.'

'We'll go the epidural,' said Ruby to Jacqueline, and bowed her head before another vicious contraction.

The anaesthetist reappeared with the same forthright manner. He stood next to Ruby, informing her of the medical limits of the epidural like a parent reading the riot act to a child. 'You're aware of what an epidural is?' Ruby nodded. 'It's a needle in the spinal cord which blocks all feeling below the waist. About one per cent of people may experience headaches afterwards, but these usually disappear in two to three weeks at the most. I have to tell you that there's a one in ten-thousand chance of more serious injury, which can mean headaches for about three months or longer. There are more remote potential complications, but I needn't go through all those with you. I've never had a patient with any problems. Are you ready to proceed?'

'Yes,' said Ruby softly.

He swung into professional action, putting on gloves, cap and gown, so that only his spectacles showed above his mouth. Jacqueline also wore a gown, and pushed a trolley laden with implements towards Ruby. He instructed Ruby to lie on her side, knees up. She turned obediently dragging the gas tube with her, as a contraction hit. She was covered in green cloth as she sweated in agony. He soaked her lower back in antiseptic. 'I'm going to give you a local anaesthetic first, so you won't feel the other needle go in. Okay?'

'Okay,' mumbled poor Ruby. Whatever, so long as the gas ball rattled we knew she was alive. Otherwise it would have appeared she was just a plaything for pain as the contractions swept through her. I don't think she felt the local anaesthetic. But she felt the rest.

What followed was the most heart-wrenching and distressing scene I have ever witnessed . . . 'I'm going to insert the needle now into the spine,' said the anaesthetist, just as a contraction hit. Ruby screamed in pain. 'You'll have to hold as still as possible,' instructed the anaesthetist. He was fiddling about where I couldn't see, and seemed to be taking a long time about it. I had to trust his professionalism. Then it all started. 'Now, I want you to tell me if you can feel the pain in your right leg,' he said, and manipulated something in Ruby's back. She screamed, her right leg kicked and her back arched.

'Right, yes!'

'Hold still.'

A contraction hit.

'Now your left leg.'

Ruby coiled like a spring as electricity shot through her legs and the contraction punched her belly.

'Left! Left!' she screamed. Her face contorted. Her hands shook. She dropped the gas, and her whole being seemed to shake.

'Right! Right leg!'

'Hold still.'

I felt absolutely helpless. My wife was in intense agony, with enormous and exhausting contraction pains, electric shocks from her womb and her spine, and only the possibility of future pain relief to comfort her. She dropped the gas tube again. I struggled to find it for her, and thrust it into her hand. She was in tears. I was close, and all I could say was, 'It'll all be over soon. The pain will go.' And had to trust that the anaesthetist would make it happen. Another midwife had suddenly appeared in the delivery suite encouraging Ruby as Jacqueline assisted the anaesthetist behind her. His face was intense as he did things out of my sight with tape, tubes and other implements. He braced Ruby's shivering side as still as possible. She seemed barely conscious in the midst of her distress, tears reddening her eyes, perspiration on her forehead, hands shaking, feet still beating the bed as the contractions bit into her curled up body. I held her hand. I stroked her arm, but we could only wait until the operation was finished and the epidural kicked in.

Finally the anaesthetist was finished. A thin tube was taped up Ruby's back from where it had been inserted into the base of her spine. It lipped over her shoulder and was secured to her gown to minimise risk of movement. From there it passed to a machine on the bench which regulated the dose of the epidural. In a flurry of green cloak and a rattle of surgical implements, the anaesthetist was suddenly gone.

It wasn't long before the epidural began taking the edge off the contractions. Jacqueline and the other midwife stayed to arrange cushions behind Ruby as she sat up. I stroked her hair, and kissed her. She looked miserable, and exhausted, but as the epidural took over, she calmed a little. The atmosphere relaxed. Ruby turned to me. 'That was terrible.'

'It was. There was nothing I could do to help you.'

'I just kept thinking of you and the baby and us as a family. That helped me get through it,' she said. What a woman, I thought, and my heart splashed inside my chest.

Jacqueline placed foetal heartbeat monitors on Ruby's belly and checked the epidural load. A hundred and forty-eight beats per minute. Seven millilitres an hour. All in order. Ruby remarked how her legs had gone numb. Jacqueline suggested we measure how far Ruby had dilated. When Ruby opened her legs they flopped uncontrollably on to the bed. No control whatsoever. I laughed. Ruby looked uncertain. Jacqueline creamed up another gloved hand and unceremoniously pushed it into Ruby's vagina.

'Seven centimetres,' she announced. 'That's good.'

That was great! Phase two of labour done! Three centimetres to go. All that pain had been effective. Four centimetres in two hours. Only three to go!

It was a waiting game from then on. The paper print-out from the monitor showed that Ruby was still undergoing violent and frequent contractions, but she felt nothing. M's heartbeat was steady. It was the chance to get some rest before the final push. I pulled the Jason recliner to the corner beside the bed. Ruby's eyes closed. A chance for a bit of respite. I leaned back in the recliner to get some rest. But the recliner kept on leaning, and I suddenly found myself upside-down with the chair on top of me, wedged in the corner, legs flailing in the air like a pair of trapped fish. I was stuck. I couldn't move. My neck was twisted in a funny angle and my arms pinned underneath me. Ruby

couldn't move to help me, or even see what had happened. I heard her ask,
'Are you okay?'
'Yes.'
'Where are you?'
'Under the bed.'
'What're you doing down there?'
'Trying to get out.'
'What happened?'
'I fell off the couch.'
'Do you want me to ring for help?'
'No.'

I paused for a moment and wondered what I should do, but decided brute force was the best approach. I shoved the chair away from me and struggled to my feet. Ruby scowled at me. 'You're supposed to be helping me.'

'I thought a laugh might do you some good,' I said. She snorted. I moved the recliner to the centre of the room.

Ruby dozed. I reclined, carefully this time, and slept.

At about 12.30 am I awoke. Ruby was still seated against her pile of cushions. Not that she could go anywhere, seeing as she had no control over her legs.

'I've been shouting at you,' she remonstrated. 'You were in such a deep sleep. I was yelling at the top of my voice.' I hadn't heard a thing. 'I need some water.'

At about 1.00 am a new midwife came in for a visit. This was Margaret, the nightshift midwife from . . . was it last night? Or the night before? Hadn't we been here an eternity? She snapped on a rubber glove and covered it with lubricant. Here we go again, I thought, have they no sense of propriety?

'Let's see how far you are,' she said, plunging her hand into Ruby's vagina. We waited, then she withdrew and announced, 'Ten centimetres.' The third phase was over. On to delivery!

My first reaction was, when will this start? In Baby School they told us that the urge to push comes naturally, but Ruby wasn't feeling it. Maybe the epidural had blocked that sensation too. Whatever the case, Ruby had to consciously start the process. She had to push the baby out, voluntarily. It's not something that just happens. Not like contractions. Contractions are the automated part of delivery, getting the hole big enough to squeeze a baby's head through. Once the hole was big enough, the mother was allowed the last role – to push the little tacker out. The contractions kept on coming though, and wouldn't let up until the baby was out. Contractions are essentially the uterus contracting. It's as if, after nine months of engorgement, the uterus has finally decided to return to its normal size, and won't stop until the blockage – the baby and all the gunk that goes with it – is expelled.

Margaret said, 'We'll turn the epidural rate down, so you can feel the contractions, but not so low that they hurt again. That way you can time the pushing with the contraction. I'll leave you here until about 2.00 am, then we can start pushing.' She reduced the epidural rate to three-and-a-half millilitres per hour and left. I suspected she had stipulated an hour because she had other patients to attend to. Whatever, it gave us another hour of dozing and rest, with perhaps a little less shouting from Ruby.

At 2.00 am Margaret returned. 'Are you ready now, dear?' she inquired, rhetorically, because she herself had determined this would be the hour. She reduced the epidural to two millilitres per hour and stood on one side of the bed. She lifted Ruby's left foot on to her hip, and instructed me to do likewise with Ruby's right foot. Turning to Ruby she said, 'Hold on to your thighs underneath, dear, and when you feel a contraction coming, push with all your strength.' I felt Ruby's foot against my hip as she pushed. Her face flushed and she grunted.

I looked to see if anything was happening, Down There. I had no idea what to expect. Nothing appeared different. She pushed another time and then a third during the contraction until it faded. Then she paused, waiting for a contraction to reappear. Mercifully, they were not painful even though she could feel them. We let her feet down. 'There's one coming,' she announced. We put her feet on our hips and she heaved again, her face purple with effort. A little widening appeared to happen, but nothing to write home about. She relaxed after three pushes. Feet down. Pause. 'One's coming.' Feet up. Push. Purple. Push. Purple. Push. Purple. A little wider. Feet down. Pause. Feet up. Push. Purple. Push. Purple. Push. Purple. A little wider. Feet down. Pause. Feet up . . . and so it went on. Ruby heaving in time with the contractions, trying to force the little head through. It was exhausting work, particularly after the day's activities before the epidural.

At one stage the midwife brought a mirror for Ruby to see what was happening. 'I'll show you the baby's head,' she said. She parted Ruby's vaginal opening. 'There it is, that grey area there, with the hair. That's baby's head.' A small circle of wrinkly grey skin, about three centimetres in diameter was visible.

Reality dropped in on us at that moment. We were going to have a baby. It sounds stupid I know: we'd seen the ultrasound, felt the movement, lived through the pregnancy, but this was somehow more tangible than before. Now we could see it. Him. Her. Ours. M. Hello M! Come on out!

Reinvigorated with the sight of her child, Ruby began really pushing.

It was not a pretty sight. Everything became distended and purple – and I mean everything from the face down to . . . where the baby is . . . and beyond. Purple face bursting with effort. Purple chest, heaving with the strain. Purple vagina, pushing out, out, out and yes, purple anus, open wide and dark. Uurgh, I didn't look too long down there. I just hoped to God it wouldn't turn inside out. Every ounce of her was pushing, pushing, pushing. I wasn't prepared for that. But what did it matter. Here was Ruby, every fibre in her opened body straining with the effort of delivery.

I was getting a bit disheartened. To my eyes nothing really seemed to be happening. With each push she would open a little, and then relax back to where it was. I doubted progress was being made. I didn't want to discourage Ruby. Margaret kept up encouraging words, announcing gradual progress with each push. But I couldn't see it, even though I didn't convey as much to Ruby. Besides, I hadn't been here before. Maybe this was a common experience according to the midwife. I suspected Ruby felt as I did because she asked for the mirror to be removed, but she didn't say so. Instead, she pushed on. Nothing else to do.

At the back of my mind I wondered what might happen if the pushing had no effect. Drugs? Caesar? I didn't know. Keep pushing Ruby!

At about three o'clock Dr Q arrived, all calm smile and easy manner. Not looking at all like he'd been woken at 3.00 am and forced to leave a warm bed for a hot delivery suite. Watching Ruby groaning with effort he summed up the state of play quickly. 'You're tired. Baby's getting distressed, not too badly, but it wants to come out. I think we'll take it out.'

No-one disagreed. We weren't quite sure how he would do it, but his confidence said it would happen, it would be all right. Maybe it was just a new member in the team, or more likely, the man who could get it done. 'I'll try suction, and give you a little episiotomy,' he said. 'Little,' I thought, that's hospital speak for a bloody big cut. Ruby was going

Reality dropped in on us at that moment. We were going to have a baby. It sounds stupid I know: we'd seen the ultrasound, felt the movement, lived through the pregnancy, but this was somehow more tangible than before. Now we could see it. Him. Her. Ours. M. Hello M! Come on out!

to be cut from vagina to anus, or pretty much. But I wasn't inclined to disagree. Nor was anyone else. Ruby was too tired, I thought it better to respect his professional judgment, and the midwife just fell in line. I wasn't mistaken though. I saw Dr Q put on a gown as Margaret wheeled the trolley of implements towards him. He reached for a pair of scissors. I could hear the snip, snip, snip, but decided not to watch. A man's got to know his limitations.

Not that the suction was any more appealing. Picture a large plastic gadget like an insulator from a high-voltage transmission line being creamed up at one end and stuffed into your wife's most intimate arena. It latches on to the baby's tiny head, and acts as a lever to yank the little thing out. Dr Q pulled on it like a dog playing with a stick. And this guy does this for a living. Thank God Ruby had an epidural. I was worried he was going to break little M's neck, but he seemed to know what he was doing. I decided this childbirth caper had reached the depths of grossness. Ruby at one end, purple with pushing, Dr Q at the other pulling on the plastic with blood pouring over the sheets. I forgot to mention the blood. As Dr Q pulled, and Ruby pushed, great ponds of blood flowed out of her womb. Poor Ruby. Miss Push-Me-Pull-You Ruby.

It took about four goes, when with a determined yank, Dr Q pulled the head through. M's head. M! Hello little M! Only a head, eyes closed, covered in gunk, just there, waiting to be pushed out. The head seemed huge! But then I realised I'd only seen just the tip of the head – the crown – inside Ruby. Now here was the full thing, poking out sideways between my wife's legs. There was a little ear, eyes tightly shut, a mat of wet dark hair and two pink little cheeks. Strangely it didn't seem odd. It was happening. M! Hello M!

Ruby paused a moment, looking down at her groin, wide-eyed and anxious. Tears were beginning to well in her eyes. Dr Q and the midwife wanted to clear M's lungs straight away, as meconium had flooded them in the womb. But they couldn't get the suction nozzle to work. Panic! I was suddenly seized with panic. This is my baby! I thought. Get it working! But I urged myself to be calm: these guys were the professionals and I had to let them do their thing. I watched in terror as Dr Q and Margaret struggled to fix the suction pipe. They tried to attach the pipe to the nozzle on the far side of the room. It wouldn't stretch. Move the bed! Margaret tried the original nozzle. Why? If it didn't work then why would it now? But it did, somehow, and I sighed in relief as they finally suctioned little M's mouth and nose.

When the moment was past, Dr Q looked up and said, 'When the next contraction comes, push and we'll get baby out.'

'I don't need a contraction,' replied Ruby. 'I can just push myself if you like.'

'Okay,' said Dr Q, still smiling his knowing, reassuring smile.

And Ruby pushed, not as hard as before, but with measured determination. I looked down over her shoulder, at the mess of implements, surgical bowls, blood and liquids, looked at little M's head and then – *Fallooloop* – a baby slipped out, all purple and white and pink and sticky, on to the sheets and the early morning gore of life. There's my M, I thought, my – my daughter, she's a girl! I've got a daughter! And she cried out. Her first breath! A certain little cry, followed by a sudden breath of air and another cry. She's breathing. What a miracle. Her lungs started in – what – a second after popping out. I've got a daughter! I watched her, for the first time, suckling on Ruby's breast. Ruby was totally absorbed, and focussed on making sure our little daughter had access to her first feed. My family. Wow.

Margaret lifted her up to Ruby who smiled and nestled with her, exhausted and deliriously happy, a new mother and new child. She was a tiny naked thing, blotched with blood and red with the effort of birth, with a mat of bloodied hair. It seemed as though the room was suddenly filled with light, as mother held child close and tears trickled down her cheeks. I have a daughter I thought.

Most of what followed was a bit of a dream. Sometime shortly after I saw Dr Q holding up what looked like someone's old jumper pulled out of the mud. 'It's the placenta,' he said. I wasn't conscious of it coming out, of whether Ruby had pushed it out, or it had just fallen out, or whether Dr Q had induced it. All I knew was I had a daughter. It was dark and pockmarked and floppy. The placenta that is. 'Nice and healthy,' said Dr Q. I saw him clamp the umbilical cord and then extract blood from it (we'd agreed to donate the cord blood). I saw the bag fill with about three-hundred millilitres of bright red liquid. I had a daughter. Sometime shortly after, I saw a pair of surgical scissors in front of me and heard Dr Q ask, 'Do you want to cut the cord?' I did – it was ceremonial in a way – the cutting of M's last link to the womb. No going back now, sweet little thing. It was surprisingly fleshy and resistant, like stiff rubber tubing. Now I know what it's like to cut human flesh. I cut between the two clamps in the cord. One clamp stays with the bub and later becomes her belly button, the other blocks the severed end of the cord. I watched Dr Q place the cord in a bowl, and then realised how much blood had been involved. Two large stainless steel bowls filled to the brim with blood and guts – the placenta swimming in it like a spent red sponge, the sheets awash with blood, some on the floor, on Margaret, on Dr Q, on Ruby, on M. I didn't check behind the bed. I was aware that Dr Q was sewing Ruby up down below, but didn't watch. It was a prettier sight next to my baby, next to my wife. So I stood and gazed at them, while Margaret and Dr Q cleared the deck. Sometime shortly after, the baby reappeared on Ruby's arm swaddled in a hospital wrap.

When all was said and done, Dr Q took our photo, we shook his hand and thanked him and he left. It was 4.00 am. Margaret took M for preliminary measurements. She weighed her. 3.4 kilograms. Measured her. Length: 52 centimetres, head circumference: 35.5 centimetres. Bathed her, to remove the blood. She squeaked and she wriggled. Most evident were her little dark eyes. She was warily looking at everything, and everyone. She didn't stop. She cried, and looked at us, as if saying, 'What is this place? Who are you? Where's the womb? Where's the breast?' Figuring it out. Bright, pink and helpless, with a whole new world to wonder at.

A Final Word

Happily destroying the myth that having a child completely ruins your sex life, our second child appeared eighteen months later when Ruby gave birth to another daughter. I note this for two reasons. First, she's as gorgeous as our first, and second, because the birth experience was so very different.

Looking back at her first birth experience, Ruby expressed disappointment about the effects of the epidural. She felt it had denied her control over the labour because it blocked her awareness of some of her body's natural processes, like the urge to push, and that it had fatigued her body by actually delaying the natural onset of the birth. She resolved to take more control over the second delivery, and was determined to draw upon the lessons she learned the first time around.

For the second labour (we called the baby 'B' this time, because B follows M in embryo) she went without any anaesthetic other than gas. She clung to me and moaned grimly as each contraction hit, but this time her focus was sharper and her determination stronger. In addition to Dr Q we had a great midwife who was a very good coach. Ruby went for the gas, breathing in and harnessing her inner strengths just before each contraction hit and clung to me as she penetrated the pain, yelling 'Here comes another one!'.

After only five hours of labour B appeared. This time I didn't hear the sound of the baby slipping into Dr Q's waiting hands. It was masked by an enormous groan from Ruby as she clung to me for one last effort, and a little girl appeared on the sheets. Ruby said afterwards that she felt we'd been a better team this time: that we'd both given birth, even though she was the one who underwent the labour. We knew more about it I suppose, and were more in control as a result.

I felt the same. I knew more about her needs, mainly because she understood the process better, so she was able to explain her needs to me beforehand. It meant I was better prepared, and more capable of helping her manage the pain. I was stronger in support both physically and emotionally and generally more attuned to her needs.

Now, from amidst the scrum of family life, I look back at those two nine-month periods with great fondness. The first pregnancy particularly was the last time I would spend with Ruby as a couple without kids. Sure, they'll grow up and leave home, but they'll always be around. Back then we only had each other and our hearts were full of excitement and apprehension. Both pregnancies were a time of great bonding for us. We were embarking on a joint project of extraordinary significance, with both awful risk and huge reward. We're lucky that no serious problems ever eventuated, and thrilled that the reward has been so great.

Australian regulations require parents to name their children within 28 days of birth. I doubt you'd be locked up if you were late, so we looked upon the 28-day period as an incentive not to leave the little girls nameless for too long. After much frantic deliberation we created names which had meanings we liked and which we thought sounded pleasing to hear. M became Mirari – meaning 'to wonder at' in Latin, from which we get the words miracle and admire. B became Amare – meaning 'to love', also a Latin word, from which the Italians get 'amore'.

Two girls, to wonder at, and to love.

A Layman's Glossary

Amniocentesis
Test for Down's Syndrome, spina bifida and other chromosomal and genetic abnormalities. It involves taking a sample of *amniotic fluid*, and is usually done around week fifteen.

Amniotic fluid
The fluid inside the *amniotic sac*, in which the *embryo* floats for nine months.

Amniotic sac
The sack containing the fluid in which the baby floats.

Blastocyst
A cluster of fertilised cells that become the *embryo* about 4–5 days after *conception*.

Braxton Hicks contraction
"False" contractions of the *uterus*. Although they are real contractions they are not repeated and do not result in *labour*.

Breech position
Baby's position at birth where the bum is turned down towards the *cervix*.

Caesar or **Caesarean section**
Surgery to remove the baby from the *womb*, via the abdomen. Named after Julius who was said to have been born that way.

Cervix
The tube between the *vagina* and the *uterus*.

Chorionic Villus Sampling
Commonly known as *CVS*. It is a test for genetic disorders involving taking a sample from the *placenta*. It can be done from about week 10 onwards.

Conception
The fusion of *sperm* and *egg* is the conception of a child.

Contraction
Repeated effort of the *uterus* which contracts in size to force the baby out. Very painful and repeated for hours on end.

Crowning
The first sight of the crown of the baby's head during delivery.

CVS
See *Chorionic Villus Sampling*.

Dilation
The *cervix* must expand up to 10 cms to allow the baby's head to pass through.

Egg See *ovum*.

Embryo
The status of the baby from just after *conception* to about week 10 or the end of the first *trimester*.

Endometrium
The lining of the *uterus*.

Epidural
Anaesthesia of the lower back, to desensitise the pain of *labour*. It involves inserting a catheter into the lower spine tissue and then drip feeding anaesthetic into it.

Episiotomy
Surgical incision beneath the *vagina* to help widen the *vagina* for delivery.

Fallopian Tubes
Tubes connecting the *ovaries* to the *uterus* – one on each side.

Father See mirror.

Fertilisation
Fusion of *sperm* and *egg* – see *conception*.

Forceps
Metal tongs sometimes used to hold a baby's head to help the doctor pull it out.

Foetus
The baby after it was an *embryo*, before it was born.

Labour
The act of giving birth. That's putting it mildly.

197

Lanugo
The covering of fine hairs on the *foetus*.

Menstruation
The woman's body's expulsion of the unfertilised *ovum* and associated uterine products each month.

Midwife
Nurse with specialist training in labour delivery and neonatal care. The best are worth their weight in gold.

Morning Sickness
Nausea associated with pregnancy, most common in the first trimester.

Mother
Goddess carrier of your child.

Nuchal Fold
A layer of fluid at the back of a *foetus'* neck. The thicker the layer, the greater the possibility of Down's Syndrome.

Nuchal Translucency
The examination of the thickness of the *nuchal fold* during an *ultrasound*.

Obstetrician
A doctor who specialises in pregnancy matters.

Ovaries
Containers at the end of each *fallopian tube* which contain the *ova*.

Ovum (ova)
The female *egg*(s) which joins(join) with the *sperm*.

Penis See *vagina*.

Placenta
The baby's nutrition pack while it is *in utero*, acting as the transmission gauge for interchange between mother and baby.

Posterior Position
The most common position of babies at birth being head towards the *vagina*, the baby's face towards mother's front.

Scrotum See below penis.

Show
The expulsion of a mucous plug from the *cervix*, which signifies the imminence of *labour*.

Sperm
The male reproductive unit which fuses with the *ovum*. See tadpole.

Testes
Incredible *sperm* production units.

Trimester
First, second or third three month block of pregnancy.

Trophoblasts
The "anchor ropes" which tie the *blastocyst* to the *uterus*, and later develop into the *amniotic sac*.

Ultrasound
Method of viewing the baby *in utero* by beaming high-frequency soundwaves into the *uterus*. Results in snowflake pictures indecipherable to all except the parents and those with medical training.

Umbilical cord
The cord joining the baby to the mother, supplying blood and nutrients and getting rid of baby waste.

Uterus
The *womb*, where the *foetus* develops.

Vagina See *penis*.

Vernix Caseosa
A waxy film on the *foetus* which develops around month five, and serves as a kind of waterproofing for the baby.

Waters
The breaching of her waters is the rupture of the *amniotic sac*, releasing the fluid through the *cervix* and *vagina*, signifying the real imminence of *labour*.

Womb See *uterus*.